The Bible, the Church, and Authority

The Canon of the Christian Bible in History and Theology

Joseph T. Lienhard, S.J.

A Michael Glazier Book

THE LITURGICAL PRESS

Collegeville, Minnesota

A Michael Glazier Book published by The Liturgical Press

Cover: Christ, the supreme teacher; 13th c. statue on the south porch of Chartres Cathedral, France.
Photo and design by Robin Pierzina, O.S.B.

2	3	4	5	6	7	8

Library of Congress Cataloging-in-Publication Data

Lienhard, Joseph T.
    The Bible, the Church, and authority : the canon of the
Christian Bible in history and theology / Joseph T. Lienhard.
        p.   cm.
    "A Michael Glazier book."
    Includes bibliographical references.
    ISBN 0-8146-5536-X
    1. Bible—Canon. 2. Bible—Evidences, authority, etc. 3. Bible—
Canon, Catholic vs. Protestant. I. Title.
BS465.L54 1995
220.1—dc20   94-44771
                                                                      CIP

For
Fr. William S. Kurz, S.J.
and
Fr. Roland J. Teske, S.J.
Priests, Scholars, Friends

Contents

Foreword

In the spring of 1989, Professor Joseph F. Kelly conveyed to me an invitation from John Carroll University to hold the Walter and Mary Tuohy Chair of Interreligious Studies there in the fall of 1992. This gracious offer gave me the chance to treat, in a new format, a topic that had long held my interest—namely, the canon of the New Testament. My attention was first drawn to it by a seminar I attended at the University of Mainz in 1972. The seminar was offered jointly by Professor Karl Suso Frank, O.F.M., of the Faculty of Catholic Theology, and Professor Ferdinand Hahn of the Faculty of Protestant Theology. Thus the interconfessional dimension of the topic was immediately clear. At least one of the papers presented in that seminar also brought out the interreligious aspect of the topic: the canonization of the New Testament had to be considered in tandem with the closing of the canon of Jewish Scriptures. Moreover, the very existence of the Septuagint—a Jewish collection of Jewish Scriptures in the Greek language, which became, for a century and a half, the Church's only Bible, and for centuries thereafter its standard Old Testament—makes the interreligious question all the more intriguing.

During the fifteen years I taught at Marquette University in Milwaukee, I offered a seminar in the history and theology of the New Testament canon several times, and when I moved to Fordham University in the Bronx, I continued to do so. In every case it has been heartening to see students begin the course expecting to learn a few names and dates and quickly master a tidy package of bare information and end it understanding some of the profound and wide-ranging theological issues that this topic raises.

The Tuohy Lectures gave me the chance to present, to a larger audience, not only some reflections on the history and theology of the canon, but also some of my own convictions about its place in the life of the Church, in Christian theology, and in ecumenical and interreligious dialogue. The lectures have been, to some extent, rearranged, revised, and expanded to make them more suitable for publication.

I gladly express my gratitude to the donors of the Tuohy Chair, Walter and Mary Tuohy; to the administrators and faculty members of John Carroll University, who invited me to give the lectures; to Professor Joseph F. Kelly, who did so much to make my stay enjoyable; to the people of the communities in Cleveland, who were such a pleasant and lively audience for these lectures; and to the graduate students at Marquette University, Fordham University, and John Carroll University whose papers, comments, and questions have led me steadily to a better understanding of the canon of the New Testament, and hence of the Word of God Himself.

Fordham University
Solemnity of St. Peter and St. Paul, 1993

Introduction

John Carroll University's oldest endowed chair, the Walter and Mary Tuohy Chair of Interreligious Studies, has as its goal ecumenical and interreligious understanding. The chair has enabled the university's department of religious studies to bring outstanding visiting scholars to campus for a semester to give classes to both undergraduate and graduate students and a series of public lectures, open to all those in greater Cleveland who are interested in the topic.

For the 1992–1993 academic year our guest was Father Joseph Lienhard, S.J., of Fordham University, whose topic was the Bible, the Church, and authority. It is difficult to find a more significant ecumenical topic than the Holy Scriptures. The Bible is central to the life of the Church, but even this centrality has not been able to eliminate a tension between the Bible and the Church, and there have even been Christians who have set the Bible against the Church. The Bible is a written document and thus unchangeable, while the Church lives in an ever-changing world. The Church wants to be faithful to the Bible and thus tries to adapt its teaching to changing times, but can this legitimate desire to make the Bible relevant result in an abandonment of the Bible's meaning? Although no Christian can imagine the Church without the Bible, all Christians must acknowledge that the Bible's role in the Church is often difficult to discern and define.

Joseph Lienhard is a specialist in Early Christianity and a well-published scholar, whose writings include another volume published by The Liturgical Press. In this volume he examines how the Christian Bible came into being, that is, how contemporary Christians know which books belong to the Bible, and he does so by casting this question against the life of the Early Christians.

x *Introduction*

This book grew out of Father Lienhard's public lectures, and John Carroll University is pleased to offer his lectures to a wider audience. But we at the university will also remember his contributions to the Tuohy Chair as a teacher and colleague during his too-short stay with us.

Joseph F. Kelly

Abbreviations

ACW	Ancient Christian Writers
ANF	Ante-Nicene Fathers
FC	Fathers of the Church
LCC	Library of Christian Classics
LCL	Loeb Classical Library
LXX	Septuagint
NAB	New American Bible
NPNF	Nicene and Post-Nicene Fathers
PL	Patrologia Latina
SC	Sources Chrétiennes

1 Pillar of Stone or Shifting Sand?

The "Problem" of the Bible

What is more certain than the Bible, an immovable pillar of stone? In the synagogue the scrolls of the Torah are given a place of highest honor. Churches display an open Bible in the sanctuary. Bound in black leather, edged in gold, the very book says "forever."

Even translations of the Bible are pillars of language. Martin Luther's version helped shape modern German. Macaulay wrote of "the English Bible, a book which, if everything else in our language should perish, would alone suffice to show the whole extent of its beauty and power."

The Bible is so much a part of our language that people quote it without realizing what they are quoting. But if you call someone the "apple of your eye," "the salt of the earth," a "fleshpot," or a "painted woman," or say he is "beside himself," you are quoting the Bible.[1] If you mention "a drop in the bucket," "the fat of the land," the "handwriting on the wall," an "olive branch," the "potter's field," the "powers that be," a "scapegoat," "sour grapes," the "strait and narrow," the "twinkling of an eye," or "wheels within wheels," you are quoting the Bible.[2] If you use

[1] "Apple of his eye": Deut 32:10; "salt of the earth": Matt 5:13; "fleshpot": Exod 16:3; "painted woman": 2 Kgs 9:30; "beside himself": Mark 3:21. These and the examples that follow are drawn from Eugene Ehrlich and David H. Scott, *Mene, Mene, Tekel* (New York: HarperCollins, 1990).

[2] "A drop in the bucket," originally "a drop of a bucket": Isa 40:15; "fat of the land": Gen 45:18; the "handwriting on the wall": Dan 5:5; "olive branch": Gen 8:11; "potter's field": Matt 27:7; "powers that be": Rom 13:1;

1

expressions like "the blind leading the blind," "face to face," "give up the ghost," "holier than thou," "hope against hope," or "keep the faith," you are quoting the Bible.[3] If you ask, "Can the leopard change his spots?" you are quoting the Bible.[4]

Every Christian denomination assures us that it rests solidly on the Bible. Protestants proudly proclaim the doctrine of *sola scriptura,* "by Scripture alone," and Catholics have enjoyed a great revival of biblical studies in the past fifty years.

Yet that pillar of stone, the Bible, seen from another angle, crumbles into a pile of shifting sand.

If you ask what books belong in the Bible, you get at least three different answers. The Protestant Old Testament is shorter than the Catholic one by seven books and parts of two more, books that Protestants call "the Apocrypha" and Catholics "deuterocanonical." And the Old Testament of the Eastern Orthodox Church is slightly longer still than the Catholic Old Testament.

But controversy over the canon, or list of books in the Bible, pales in comparison with controversy over its interpretation. In the United States today, perhaps the biggest Bible-reading nation in the world, every line on the spectrum is represented. Some Christians insist that every word of the Bible is literally true: God did make the world in six days, the sun did stand still for Joshua, Jonah did live in the belly of a whale for three days. The controversy over teaching evolution in public schools is far from over, and "creation science" has more than a few advocates. Some Christians even handle poisonous snakes to prove the truth of Mark 16:18.

Or did Ira Gershwin have it right in *Porgy and Bess* when he wrote:

> It ain't necessarily so—
> The things that you're liable
> To read in the Bible—
> It ain't necessarily so.

"scapegoat": Lev 16:8; "sour grapes": Ezra 18:2; "strait and narrow": Matt 7:14; "twinkling of an eye": 1 Cor 15:52; "wheels within wheels": Ezra 1:16.

[3] "The blind leading the blind": Matt 15:14; "face to face": Exod 33:11; "give up the ghost": Mark 15:39; "holier than thou": Isa 65:5; "hope against hope": Rom 4:18; "keep the faith": 2 Tim 4:7.

[4] Jer 13:23.

Montesquieu, in his *Persian Letters,* has his traveller visit a Catholic monastery, where a friendly father librarian gives the Persian guest a tour. The visitor speaks:

> "Father," I said, "what are those fat volumes which fill the whole side of the library?"
>
> "Those," he replied, "are interpretations of Scripture."
>
> "There are certainly many of them," I answered. "The Scripture must have been most obscure once, but very clear now. Do any doubts remain? Can there still be any contested points?"[5]

The librarian, of course, blushes and explains that the interpretations only gave rise to more, and more bitter, controversies. William Blake summed up the situation more succinctly:

> Both read the Bible day and night,
> But thou read'st black where I read white.

Interestingly, these lines come from a poem entitled *The Everlasting Gospel,* and the contrast between the Bible and the Gospel will come up again.

The Christian Bible raises another problem. More than three-fourths of it,[6] the Christian Old Testament, is identical with the sacred scriptures of the Jews and consists of books written before Jesus of Nazareth was born, books which never once mention Jesus. The Christian use of the Jewish Scriptures has rightly been called the biggest corporate takeover in history. This fact is so well known that it has ceased to surprise or even interest most people, and that is unfortunate.

These introductory considerations bring us nearer to the purpose of the Tuohy Chair. According to the benefactors, Walter and

---

[5] Montesquieu, *The Persian Letters,* Letter cxxxiv, Rica to—, trans. George R. Healy (Indianapolis: Bobbs-Merrill, 1964) 229.

[6] In *The New Oxford Annotated Bible with the Apocrypha* (New York: Oxford, 1973), the Old Testament has 1,163 pages, the New Testament 344, and the "Apocrypha" 293. Hence in the Protestant canon, the Old Testament is roughly 77 percent of the Bible and the New Testament 23 percent. Not all the books printed among the "Apocrypha" are in the Catholic canon; about 231 pages are. In the Catholic canon, the ratio of Old Testament to New Testament is about 80 percent to 20 percent.

Mary Tuohy, these lectures are to deal with interreligious studies. The Bible, or a part of it, constitutes a crucial meeting place for Catholics, Jews, the Orthodox, and Protestants. This meeting place has a long, and sometimes painful, history, and monuments to many battles can be seen there. Sometimes the meeting place is bathed in clear and beautiful light, but more often it is obscured by dark, even ominous shadows. I hope, in the course of these lectures, to approach that meeting place from several different paths and to ponder both the light and the shadows.

A prenote is appropriate here. I am a Catholic, and terms that I use express my Catholic faith. I intend no less and no more than honesty. To express one's own faith is surely not to offend another.

What makes problems with the Bible so acute, of course, is the fact that, for the Church, as for the Synagogue, the Bible has not only authority, but divine authority. These lectures are entitled: "The Bible, the Church, and Authority." They are meant to explore the complex relations among all three.

I have mentioned several "problems" with the Bible. One more remains to be mentioned—one that, in our time, towers above all others. It concerns, not the interpretation of this or that part of the Bible, but the far more important question, where the truth of the Bible is to be found. For more than a century—somewhat less in Catholic circles—the prevailing method for interpreting the Bible has been the historical method. The historical method locates the truth of the Bible primarily in the past: what any passage means is what its human author intended it to mean. The historical method claims for itself "objectivity"; and as a sign of its objectivity, its activity is often called "biblical studies." Historicism— the theory behind the historical method—arose in response to Kant's criticism of assumed certainties. It was applied first to secular subjects, and then, from the early part of the nineteenth century on, to the study of the Bible and other ancient religious texts. Gertrude Himmelfarb has described historicism as "a form of relativism that locates the meaning of ideas and events so firmly in their historical context that history, rather than philosophy and nature, becomes the arbiter of truth."[7]

---

[7] Gertrude Himmelfarb, "Tradition and Creativity in the Writing of History," *First Things*, n. 27 (November 1992) 28.

The historical method has surely shed much light on the meaning of the Scriptures. But its application to the sacred books raises problems. These problems arise from the claim, made by extreme historicism, not only to objectivity, but to exclusive objectivity.

The Bible is the Church's book, and believers want to know what the Bible means for them, now. Origen, in a sermon he preached on the Book of Genesis early in the third century, drew the contrast about as succinctly as anyone could. He got to Genesis 18:8, "And [Abraham] stood . . . under the tree," and remarked: "We ought not believe that it was of greatest concern to the Holy Spirit to write in the books of the Law where Abraham was standing. For what does it help me who have come to hear what the Holy Spirit teaches the human race, if I hear that 'Abraham was standing . . . under a tree'?"[8]

Like Origen, modern believers want "to hear what the Holy Spirit teaches." The historical method, wrongly applied, appears to separate the "true meaning" of a text from its doctrinal meaning, its meaning in the Church for believers.

Jon D. Levenson has been concerned with this problem for some time, and I gratefully borrow from what he has written.[9]

An appeal to "objectivity" is found in a recent book that has attracted considerable attention, John P. Meier's *A Marginal Jew*.[10] Meier writes: "My method follows a simple rule: it prescinds from what Christian faith or later Church teaching says about Jesus."[11] The easy parallelism between faith and doctrine begs for further comment, but I move on to an intriguing sentence: "Suppose that a Catholic, a Protestant, a Jew, and an agnostic . . . were locked in the bowels of the Harvard Divinity School library, put on a spartan diet, and not allowed to emerge until they had hammered out a consensus document on who Jesus of Nazareth was and what

---

[8] *Homilies on Genesis* 4, 3, trans. Ronald E. Heine, FC 71 (Washington: The Catholic University of America, 1982) 106.

[9] "Theological Consensus or Historicist Evasion? Jews and Christians in Biblical Studies," in *Hebrew Bible or Old Testament? Studying the Bible in Judaism and Christianity*, ed. Roger Brooks and John J. Collins; *Christianity and Judaism in Antiquity*, 5 (Notre Dame: University of Notre Dame, 1990) 109–145.

[10] John P. Meier, *A Marginal Jew: Rethinking the Historical Jesus* (New York: Doubleday, 1991).

[11] Ibid., 1.

he intended in his own time and place. An essential requirement of this document would be that it be based on purely historical sources and arguments."[12]

A passage in Chaim Potok's novel *In the Beginning* yields a very different perspective. David Lurie is a yeshiva student about to be ordained. He tells his father, Max, that he has applied for admission to a university to pursue biblical studies. Max Lurie, David's father, speaks first:[13]

> "Tell me what it means to study Bible in a university. Your teachers will be goyim [Gentiles]?"
>
> "And Jews."
>
> "The Jews are observers of the commandments?"
>
> "I don't know. They may be. I'm not certain."
>
> "It is unimportant to you that they may not be observers of the commandments? . . . You will study Torah with goyim and with Jews who are like goyim? What do they know of the Torah?"

Of course, Max Lurie's words might be taken as the words of a narrow-minded sectarian. Every religious body has its sub-groups who insist that they, and only they, have all the right answers. Most of us could name several such groups without much effort.

But Max Lurie's words are not the words of a bigot. He wants his son to study, not with Jews, but with observant Jews.

John Meier gathers a Catholic, a Protestant, a Jew, and an agnostic to write about Jesus. It is the agnostic, of course, who makes the rules. The Catholic, the Protestant, and the Jew, to the extent that they follow the rules, are not that, but something else.

John Meier and Max Lurie differ on how they understand the relation of commitment and truth. Meier's scholars prescind from their faith; Max Lurie believes that only those who live the Torah can know the Torah. And there are some sorts of knowledge that can only follow commitment, love, and risk. The absurdity of a young man saying to a young woman, "I would like, first, to know everything about you that can be known, and then I shall decide whether or not I love you," is patent. The same is true of the Bible.

---

[12] Ibid.

[13] Chaim Potok, *In the Beginning* (New York: Fawcett Crest, 1976) 423.

Thus the first problem with the historical method: of itself, it can only affirm discrete facts from the past. As such, it cannot provide the foundation for faith. Two choices remain: either to abandon faith, or to fall into fideism.

Another problem with the historical method is that it is not quite as objective as it claims to be. Again, Levenson has articulated this point particularly well. He quotes James Kugel, who wrote that the modern study of the Bible, "from its inception, . . . was fundamentally a Protestant undertaking, one might even say, a form of Protestant piety."[14] For example, the secession of the Northern Kingdom in the tenth century B.C. is interpreted as the rejection of entrenched power, including a religious hierarchy, and the establishment of decentralized worship—a kind of anticipation of the Protestant Reformation that occurred two and a half millennia later. Relative lack of interest in the cult, and in the post-exilic books, betrays a "preference for prophet over priest, for the word over the sacrament, and for the spirit over institutional structures."[15] Authors quietly assume that Israelite religion degenerated into Judaism, which Jesus could then either reform or reject.

A Catholic might raise similar questions about the framework of New Testament studies, even using Kugel's words: is there a "preference for prophet over priest, for the word over the sacrament, and for the spirit over institutional structures"?

To give one example, there is a category common in German Protestant thought—so common that it has been used for almost a century without explanation; it is "early Catholicism," in German *Frühkatholizismus.* The word is not often used in English, but its effects are often visible. The term originated with Ferdinand Christian Baur, who taught in Tübingen in the first half of the nineteenth century. Baur tried to understand the history of the early Church by applying Hegel's dialectical categories to it. He held that the thesis is Jewish Christianity, represented by James, the antithesis Gentile Christianity, represented by Paul, and the synthesis "early Catholicism." Hence he understood Catholicism as Pauline Christianity that has recombined, to some extent, with Judaism. Another German scholar, Adolf von Harnack, defined

---

[14] James L. Kugel, "Biblical Studies and Jewish Studies," *Association for Jewish Studies Newsletter* 36 (1986) 22.

[15] Levenson, "Theological Consensus," 113.

the three characteristics of early Catholicism as these: a canon of Scripture, the rule of faith, and the monepiscopate (that is, having one bishop as the head of each local Church).

But to say that Catholicism is Christianity that has recombined with Judaism degrades both Catholicism and Judaism. Moreover, to say that a period existed in which pure Christianity, which had not yet declined into Catholicism, existed, is to erect a wall right through the history of early Christianity and to divide it into an early, ideal state and a later, degraded state. The characteristics of the later state are the New Testament, dogma, and a hierarchy. The theory presupposes that Christianity can and did exist without these elements.

What is the point? I do not deny the validity of historical studies of the Bible; we have learned a great deal from such studies. But I offer three cautions. First: the idea that one can put aside religious faith and thereby obtain objectivity should be questioned on several points—what it implies about the relation of faith to the person, and what sort of "objectivity" is thus attained. Second: the appeal of any Sacred Scriptures is the firm belief that in them, God speaks to the believer. If historical studies prescind from such belief they are, to that extent, out of touch with believers. And finally, historical biblical studies may not be as objective as they sometimes claim to be; in particular, they have often been slanted toward Protestant presuppositions and against Judaism and Catholicism.

Thus, I believe, the rise of historicism and of the historical method makes the question of the canon particularly acute in our day. The consideration of the canon—which, at first, may seem to be a dry exercise, repeating what has long been known and settled—turns out to be anything but that. Few other questions in modern theology have so many implications: biblical studies, scriptural theology, historical theology, systematic theology, and even liturgy all have a stake in the question of the canon. In the lectures that follow, I hope to answer a few questions about the canon and—even more—to provoke further questions.

2 Jewish Scriptures or Old Testament?

The Church's First Bible

Twenty-five years after the first Easter, St. Paul wrote this to the Christians at Corinth:

> I delivered to you as of first importance what I also received, that Christ died for our sins in accordance with the scriptures, that he was buried, that he was raised on the third day in accordance with the scriptures, and that he appeared to Cephas, then to the twelve (1 Cor 15:3-5).

"Christ died for our sins," Paul writes, and "he was raised on the third day"—and both events took place "in accordance with the scriptures." Nowhere do the Scriptures—for Paul, of course, the Jewish Scriptures—explicitly state that "Christ died for our sins" or that "he was raised on the third day." Yet Paul is convinced that they do so implicitly. In other words, Paul assumes that he interprets the Scriptures correctly, and that the correct interpretation goes beyond the strictly literal sense. On this point he is one with almost all early Christians.[1]

As already noted, more than three-fourths of the Christian Bible is identical with the Sacred Scriptures of the Jews—books written

---

[1] To quote only one other example, Jesus' words to the two disciples on the road to Emmaus (Luke 24:25-27): "And he said to them, 'O foolish men, and slow of heart to believe all that the prophets have spoken! Was it not necessary that the Christ should suffer these things and enter into his glory?' And beginning with Moses and all the prophets, he interpreted to them in all the scriptures the things concerning himself."

before Jesus of Nazareth was born, books that never mention Jesus. Thus the question raised here: Was this Bible the Jewish Scriptures, as the Jews claimed, or was it the "Old Testament," as the Christians claimed? The answer hinges, of course, on "interpretation," in this case how the Christians' interpretation of the Jewish Scriptures made those Scriptures their "Old Testament."

Before considering the Bible, it is worth reflecting on what "interpretation" means in itself. The word comes from a Latin noun that means "go-between," "advocate," or "translator." An interpreter "goes between" something that is not understood—speech, writing, or art, for example—and a person who does not understand it but wants to. Interpreters translate from one language to another. They also explain what is obscure: Blake's poetry or Picasso's paintings. The White House press office is often busy issuing interpretations.

To ask for an interpretation involves both trust and risk: I have to trust that the interpreter knows his business, and I risk getting a wrong interpretation. Insofar as an interpreter says: "I understand, and you don't," he exercises a form of authority. But authority, unlike power, does not exclude freedom: I can always say, "I'll get another interpretation." Since I can say that, it follows that accepting an interpretation can imply having a norm for judging whether it is a good one.

It is often worth asking whether I need an interpreter. If someone is speaking Russian or Chinese to me, I surely do. But sometimes we should trust ourselves. Someone who has never been to an art museum may go into a great marble building, walk into a gallery room, and see a painting that looks very much like a bunch of asparagus. He may think that no one would hang a picture of a bunch of asparagus in such an awe-inspiring place and, instead of saying, "that looks like a bunch of asparagus," say, "I don't understand. Could someone explain it to me?" People who tell us, "You don't understand," sometimes mean "You don't see it my way."

The obvious meaning is often a fine starting point. The story is told of a famous professor of New Testament at an equally famous divinity school. He was lecturing on Paul's Letter to the Romans and came to a particularly difficult verse. In a brilliant lecture he succinctly explained the twelve most important theories of how the verse should be interpreted, all in forty-nine minutes and fifty seconds. And then, as the class was about to end, he looked up from his notes and said, "And in thirteenth and last place, it may mean exactly what it says."

I also like the story of a group of poor but devout Christian women in the South. For years and years they met every Sunday afternoon, sat around a kitchen table, and read the Bible to each other. An outsider once asked them, "What do you do when you get to a difficult passage?" One of the women thought for a while and answered, "Well, we explain it to each other."

Interpretation among Greeks and Jews

The Christian interpretation of the Jewish Scriptures involved both trust and risk, and had its own clear norm—a point we will return to. But the interpretation of a sacred text was not a Christian invention. Greek philosophers had employed interpretation and reflected on it; and, by Jesus' time, Jews had established several traditions of interpretation.

Greek myths and epic poems told of gods and goddesses with enormous appetites for food, for drink, and for each other. Eventually these myths became embarrassing. They might simply be banned, as Plato tried to ban the poets from his ideal republic, or they could be "interpreted"—that is, their "true meaning" sought.

The Stoic philosophers, in particular, practiced the art of interpreting the old myths and discovering, hidden beneath the narrative, noble Stoic principles. The fourth-century philosopher Sallustius wrote: "the soul should, through the seeming strangeness, consider the words to be veils and believe the truth to be beyond speech."[2]

For Jews, the interpretation of the Bible was a far more serious undertaking than the Stoics' efforts to save Homer. The Greeks

---

[2] Quoted by C. K. Barrett, "The Interpretation of the Old Testament in the New," in *Cambridge History of the Bible,* I: *From the Beginnings to Jerome,* ed. P. R. Ackroyd and C. F. Evans (Cambridge: University Press, 1970) 379. The compete quotation is: "Why have they told in their myths of adulteries and thefts and the binding of fathers and other strange things? Or is this also worthy to be marvelled at, that the soul should, through the seeming strangeness, consider the words to be veils and believe the truth to be beyond speech." Sallustius, *De diis et mundo liber,* 3 (F.W.A. Mullach, ed., *Fragmenta Philosophorum Graecorum,* 3 [Paris: Firmin-Didot, 1928] 31).

considered Homer to be culturally sacred. The Jews understood the Torah as sacred in a far deeper sense: it was God's own word to His people.

Three different styles of Jewish interpretation existed around the time of Jesus.[3]

Alexandrian Judaism saw the Scriptures as the source of profound philosophical teaching. This tendency was already present in the Septuagint and reached its full flowering in Philo of Alexandria (ca. 20 B.C. to ca. A.D. 50), who was roughly a contemporary of Jesus'. Philo wrote extensively on the Torah, the first five books of the Bible, and discovered there the teachings of contemporary Alexandrian Platonic philosophy. Philo wanted some laws, like the law of the Sabbath, to be observed literally;[4] but other passages, he insisted, could not be taken literally: for example, that a woman came out of Adam's side;[5] that God planted vines and olive trees and fruit trees;[6] or that God has a face.[7] To explain these passages, Philo recommended "the path through allegory."[8]

"Allegory" is a bad word for many contemporaries, who take it to be simply "making the text mean whatever you want it to mean"; bizarre examples can easily be cited. But Philo worked from clear principles. The most basic one was this: the meaning of the text had to be worthy of its author, and its author is God. If the surface meaning seemed unworthy of God, then the true meaning had to be sought beyond the veil of speech.

The Palestinian rabbis had a very different sort of interpretation. They accepted the Scripture as the record of God's revealed will for the conduct of Jewish life. The Scripture was Law, and God did not change or abrogate his Law. If circumstances changed, then solutions to new problems had to be found, and they were found

---

[3] Some of what follows is drawn from Barrett, "The Interpretation of the Old Testament."

[4] See, for example, *The Decalogue* and *The Special Laws*.

[5] *Allegories of the Laws* 2, 7, 19 (LCL Philo 1, 236, 238).

[6] *On the Planting* 8, 32 (LCL Philo 3, 288).

[7] *On Cain's Posterity* 1, 1 (LCL Philo 2, 328).

[8] Ibid., 1, 7 (LCL Philo 2, 330). Philo knew that he was not the first allegorist, and even knew of rules or principles for it; he uses the phrase "the rules of allegory" in *On Dreams* 1, 73 (LCL Philo 5, 334).

in interpreting the Law. Passages that seemed contradictory, or unworthy of God, also called for interpretation.[9]

The Jewish community of the Dead Sea scrolls engaged in yet another sort of interpretation. They were convinced that they lived in the last age, and that the Scriptures were being fulfilled in them and in what happened to them. Philo and the rabbis had focused their attention on the Torah. The authors of the Dead Sea scrolls focused rather on the prophets, and on that point they were closer to the Christians. They believed that the prophets wrote not about their own time but about the end-time, and that they, the community, lived in the end-time. They themselves, and their deeds, were the fulfillment of Scripture.[10] There is a parallel in Jesus' words in the synagogue at Nazareth; after the reading of Isaiah he said: "Today this scripture has been fulfilled in your hearing" (Luke 4:21).

In the Jewish Scriptures Philo found the best philosophy, the rabbis found the God-given basis for a system of law, and the community at Qumran found prophecies of itself. And each believed that they had discovered the true meaning of the Scriptures, the truth beyond the speech, as Sallustius had written.

Were they wrong? Were they simply "reading into" the Scriptures?

The question, "Were they right or wrong?" is not especially helpful. Modern readers often assume that the literal, original sense of a text is its "true" meaning, and that any other understanding is somehow a departure from the true meaning. Religious writers of late antiquity—whether they were pagans, Jews, or Christians—assumed the opposite: that the words were veils, and that the truth lay beyond the words. Jews and Christians also believed that the Scripture was the word of God and that, as such, it spoke to them about what was most important. Each of the three Jewish groups mentioned came to the Scriptures with its own convictions about what was important: truth or God's will for right living or prophecy of the approaching end. The Christians, as we shall see, ap-

---

[9] Of course, the rabbis were concerned with more than law, and expanded many parts of the Scripture as homilies or speculation, in *haggadah*. Some scholars have even written of rabbinic mysticism.

[10] See Barrett, "Interpretation of the Old Testament," 389.

proached the Scriptures with a markedly different conviction about what was most important.

Interpretation in the New Testament

Most of the New Testament authors were Jews, and the three sorts of Jewish interpretation can all be found in the New Testament.

Philo's quest for philosophical truth is the least common, but the use of the adjective "true" in John's Gospel, where Jesus is the true light, the true bread, the true vine,[11] is noteworthy.

New Testament books also show the Scriptures being used to establish rules.[12] One clear instance is the discussion of divorce in Mark 10:2-12. The Pharisees summarize Deuteronomy 24:1 to show that Moses permitted divorce. Jesus quotes Genesis 1:27 and 5:2 against them, and argues that Moses' permitting divorce was an exception granted "for your hardness of heart" (Mark 10:5), whereas the passages from Genesis indicate God's will "from the beginning of creation" (Mark 10:6). One author speculates that, had this sort of interpretation continued, a Christian Mishnah might have resulted.[13]

The way the community of the Dead Sea scrolls understood the Scriptures—that is, as prophecy—has the most striking parallels in the New Testament. The evangelists, for example, believed that the Scriptures foretold even details of Jesus' life. In the first two chapters of St. Matthew's Gospel, the virginal conception of Jesus, his birth in Bethlehem, the slaughter of the innocents, and Jesus' dwelling in Nazareth are all seen as the fulfillment of prophecies.[14] St. John does the same when he writes of Jesus' Passion: when

[11] See ibid., 401–402.

[12] Soon to be called laws; the phrase "the new law" occurs for the first time in the *Epistle of Barnabas* 2, 6.

[13] Greer in James L. Kugel and Rowan A. Greer, *Early Biblical Interpretation* (Philadelphia: Westminster, 1986) 129.

[14] Matt 1:22-23, quoting Isa 7:14; Matt 2:5-6, quoting Mic 5:2; Matt 2:17-18, quoting Jer 31:15; and Matt 2:23, quoting a phrase not found in the Old Testament.

the soldiers cast lots for Jesus' cloak, when Jesus' legs are not broken, or when his side is pierced, a prophecy is fulfilled.[15]

New Testament authors employ other patterns besides prophecy and fulfillment. One is type and antitype, or model and its realization. Moses' lifting up the serpent in the wilderness to save the people from death is a type of Jesus exalted on the cross.[16] Jonah's three days in the belly of a fish are a type of Christ's three days in the tomb.[17] Noah's salvation through water is a type of Christian baptism.[18]

Another pattern found occasionally in the New Testament is allegory. Paul makes explicit use of it in the Letter to the Galatians, where Abraham's two children stand allegorically for Jews and Gentiles.[19]

We have seen how different ways of interpreting the Scriptures appear in the New Testament. But we have not yet penetrated to the heart of the matter. What allowed the new believers, the Christians, to use the Jewish Scriptures at all? The answer is very simple, and its explanation is very complex. The answer is this: the Christians believed that Jesus Christ is the key to understanding the Scriptures.[20] The explanation we will see only gradually.

Three Solutions That Failed

The earliest Christians accepted the Jewish Scriptures as their own because they found in these Scriptures confirmation of their faith in Christ. But the passages that they appealed to were only a small fraction of the whole Bible. Then a rude awakening took place. Once the Christians had taken the Jewish Scriptures as their own, they had to come to terms with the whole of these Scriptures: not just with a few passages that confirmed their faith, but with great masses of law and cultic regulations, histories of obscure persons, genealogies, prophecies about enemies long dead, foreign-

---

[15] John 19:24, quoting Ps 22:18; John 19:36, quoting Exod 12:46; John 19:37, quoting Zech 12:10.

[16] Num 21:9 and John 3:14.

[17] Jonah 1:17 and Matt 12:40.

[18] Gen 6-8 and 1 Pet 3:20.

[19] See Gal 4:22-31.

[20] See 2 Cor 3:12-18.

sounding wisdom literature, and the hymn-book of the second temple.

Around the middle of the second century, several Christians faced up to the problem of the Old Testament in the Church in a systematic fashion.

A man named Marcion of Pontus represents one extreme. Around A.D. 140, after he made a fortune in the shipping business, he moved from Pontus, in Asia Minor, to Rome. He joined the Christian Church there, and gave its leaders a large gift of money. Four years later the Church at Rome excommunicated him as a heretic and, interestingly, gave him his money back.

Marcion read the Old Testament and was appalled.[21] There he read about an inferior god, a god who was so ignorant that he could not find Adam, and had to ask, "Where are you?" (Gen 3:9); a god who was so inconsistent that he first commanded Moses not to make images, then told him to make a bronze serpent; and a god who was so vicious that he ordered the most awful slaughters of women and children. In other words, Marcion read the Old Testament, accepted every word of it as literally true, and drew a logical, if radical, conclusion: the Old Testament must be thrown out of the Church, for it and its god are unworthy of Christianity. In Jesus an entirely new revelation had taken place—so new that it was the work of a hitherto unknown God. Thus Marcion postulated two gods. One, the inferior god of justice, the god of the Old Testament, was the creator of the world. The other, the higher God of love, was the Father of Jesus Christ. The Jewish Scriptures recorded the doings of the inferior, creator god.

Marcionism, in mitigated forms, remains a temptation for Christians—and for others, too. Thomas Paine, the political propagandist of the American Revolution, once wrote:

> Whenever we read the obscene stories, the voluptuous debaucheries, the cruel and tortuous executions, the unrelenting vindictiveness with which more than half the Bible is filled, it would be more consistent that we call it the word of a demon than the word of God. It is a history of wickedness that has served to corrupt and brutalize mankind.

[21] For the examples see Hendrik F. Stander, "Marcion," in *Encyclopedia of Early Christianity,* ed. Everett Ferguson et al. (New York and London: Garland, 1990) 568–569.

The best-known book on Marcion ever published was the work of Adolf von Harnack (1851–1930), the brilliant and original, if idiosyncratic, historian of early Christianity. Harnack found in Marcion a kindred spirit. Toward the end of the book he made a famous statement:

> To reject the Old Testament in the second century was an error that the great Church rightly rejected. To retain it in the sixteenth century was a fate that the Reformation was not yet capable of escaping. But to keep it, since the nineteenth century, as a canonical document in Protestantism is the consequence of religious and ecclesiastical paralysis.[22]

If Marcion denied that the Old Testament had anything to do with Christianity, the author of a document called the *Epistle of Barnabas,* probably written about 140 in Alexandria in Egypt, made the opposite claim.[23]

Barnabas (to use the author's familiar pseudonym), like Marcion, denies any positive relation between the Jews of the Old Testament and the Church. But from there on they part ways. Marcion taught that the Old Testament was an exclusively Jewish book, and hence useless to the Church. Barnabas held that the Old Testament was an exclusively Christian book. If Marcion took the Old Testament perfectly literally and threw it out of the Church, Barnabas took it exclusively figuratively and took it away from the Synagogue.

Barnabas's theory is this: the Jews lost the covenant immediately after Moses received it. Moses received the covenant on Mount Sinai, and the Jews lost it when they worshipped the golden calf.[24] And further, the Jews made a fateful error: they listened to a wicked angel and interpreted their Scriptures literally.[25]

---

[22] Adolf von Harnack, *Marcion: Das Evangelium vom fremden Gott. Eine Monographie zur Geschichte der Grundlegung der katholischen Kirche* (Leipzig: J. C. Hinrichs, 1924) 217. The book has been translated into English: *Marcion: The Gospel of the Alien God,* trans. John E. Steely and Lyle D. Bierma (Durham: Labyrinth, 1990).

[23] English translations are available in most collections of the Apostolic Fathers, for example *The Apostolic Fathers* I, trans. Kirsopp Lake, LCL (orig. publ. 1912; repr. Cambridge: Harvard, 1975).

[24] *Epistle of Barnabas* 4, 6–8; 14, 1–4.

[25] Ibid., 9, 4.

Barnabas then goes on to give examples of the true interpretation of the Scriptures. A few examples should suffice. When Scripture says that Abraham circumcised 318 members of his household, it was really making a prophecy of Christ, for the Greek number 18 is the first two letters of the name "Jesus," and 300 is the letter tau (T), a picture of the cross.[26] (The fact that the Scriptures were written in Hebrew, not Greek, does not slow Barnabas down for a moment.) The prohibition against eating pork really means avoiding men who pray to God only when they are in need, for pigs ignore their owners when they are feeding, but bellow when they are hungry.[27] The prohibitions against eating rabbits, hyenas, and weasels are really prohibitions against deviant sexual sins,[28] while the commandment of kosher, to eat animals that chew the cud and have a cloven hoof,[29] means associating only with people who meditate on the Lord and his commandments, and who have one foot on earth and one in heaven.[30]

A few decades after Marcion and Barnabas wrote, a Gnostic, Ptolemy, addressed a letter to a woman named Flora and again encountered the problem of the Old Testament. Gnosticism was a kind of theosophy that one scholar has called "Platonism for people who can't read." Most Gnostic writings are obscure in the extreme, but Ptolemy's letter is an exception. It is not only clear, but seductive in its answer to the "problem" of the Old Testament in the Church.[31]

Ptolemy's topic is how to understand "the law ordained through Moses." Like any middling-good teacher, he excludes two extremes so that he can portray himself as a moderate. The extremes are these: either the law was laid down by God the Father, or the adversary, the destructive devil, ordained it.[32] Neither, of course, is true: the Law is imperfect, but it does prohibit injustice.[33]

[26] Ibid., 9, 7.

[27] Ibid., 10, 3. Such an allegorical interpretation of the dietary laws was already anticipated in the *Letter of Aristeas*.

[28] Ibid., 10, 6–8.

[29] Lev 11:3; Deut 14:6.

[30] *Epistle of Barnabas*. 10, 10–11.

[31] Preserved by Epiphanius, *Panarion* 33. A convenient translation is available in Karlfried Froelich, ed., *Biblical Interpretation in the Early Church,* Sources of Early Christian Thought (Philadelphia: Fortress, 1984) 37–43, which is quoted here.

[32] *Letter of Ptolemy* 3, 2.

[33] Ibid., 3, 4–5.

Ptolemy then, in a remarkably modern turn, undertakes a kind of source criticism. There is not one lawgiver, but three: God himself, Moses, and the elders of the people. Moses was not speaking for God when he wrote, but recorded his own reflections; and the elders introduced some precepts on their own authority.[34] Ptolemy proves his point from Jesus' own words: Jesus taught that God legislated the permanence of marriage, and said that Moses allowed divorce as an exception.[35] In another passage, Jesus rejects the tradition of the elders on denying support owed to parents by an appeal to *korban*.[36]

Ptolemy divides the law ordained by God into three classes. The first is "the pure legislation not entangled with evil," which Christ came not to abolish but to fulfill; an example is the Decalogue. The second is legislation "entangled with the inferior and with injustice"; this the Savior abolished. An example is the *lex talionis*, "an eye for an eye." The third class is "typological and symbolic legislation ordained in the image of spiritual and higher things."[37] Examples abound for Ptolemy: "sacrifices, circumcision, the Sabbath, fasting, the Passover, unleavened bread."[38] These were images and symbols. When the truth was revealed, their practice was abolished, but their spiritual meaning remained.[39]

The Church excommunicated Marcion and condemned Marcionism. Barnabas found no disciples. Ptolemy's principles were rejected. Generally, the early Church did not define its teachings on its own initiative. Instead, it defined them by reacting. Only when someone announced, "I've got it all figured out," did the Church take a long look at the solution, measure it against its sense of the faith, and often enough say, "No, you don't; that's not in line with our faith." Thus, in rejecting Marcion as a heretic, in not following Barnabas, and in not accepting Ptolemy's principles, the Church made some important affirmations.

[34] Ibid., 4, 1–3.
[35] Ibid., 4, 4, quoting Matt 19:8 and 6.
[36] Ibid., 4, 11–13 quoting Matt 15:6-9.
[37] Ibid., 5, 1-2; cf. Matt 5:17, 38.
[38] Ibid., 5, 8.
[39] "All of these were images and symbols, and as such they underwent a transformation when the truth was made manifest. In terms of outward appearance and external performance they were abolished, but in terms of spiritual significance they were lifted up. The words remained, but the contents were changed" (ibid., 5, 9).

By rejecting Marcion, the Church affirmed that there is only one God. The God of the Old Testament is the Father of Jesus Christ, and the Jewish Scriptures are the true word of the one true God. Divine justice and divine love do not exclude each other. More than two centuries after Marcion, a council at Constantinople formulated a creed, perhaps the most ecumenical creed in Christianity. Catholics know it from Sunday Mass. In the article beginning "We believe in the Holy Spirit," this creed affirms that "he spoke through the prophets." These are the Church's final words against Marcion: the Holy Spirit of God also inspired the Old Testament.

By rejecting Barnabas the Church affirmed that the Old Testament has a literal sense, and that the literal sense is true. God did make a covenant with Israel, and Israel understood the covenant and lived it.

By rejecting Ptolemy's principles, the Church affirmed that the whole Old Testament is the word of the one true God and contains nothing that is inferior or unjust.

The Orthodox Response: Irenaeus of Lyons

In rejecting Marcion, Barnabas, and Ptolemy, the Church implicitly affirmed some important teachings or doctrines. But doctrine is not yet theology. The first coherent theological thought about the place of the Old Testament in the Church came from Irenaeus, a bishop of Lyons in what is now southeastern France.[40] Irenaeus had come from the East, served as a priest in Lyons, and shortly before 180 was elected bishop there. His predecessor had been martyred, so the job qualified as hazardous duty. But Irenaeus considered the real enemy, not the lions in the arena, but the Gnostics, and wrote a large book about them with the decidedly clear title, *The Unmasking and Overthrow of the Falsely-Named "Knowledge"*—usually called simply *Against the Heresies*. In one scholar's opinion, this book marks the dawn of theology.[41]

[40] Greer's study of Irenaeus in Kugel and Greer, *Early Biblical Interpretation,* has been helpful for this section.

[41] "L'apparition de la théologie," the words of J. Lebreton cited by Lucien Regnault, "Irénée de Lyon," *Dictionnaire de spiritualité ascétique et mystique* 7 (1971) 1939.

Marcion, Barnabas, and Ptolemy had each postulated a disjunction between creation and redemption, between the Old Testament and Christ. Irenaeus refused to turn the history of the world into two opposing metaphysical principles. Instead, he affirmed the continuity of creation and redemption. There is one God, Irenaeus insists, and that one God is both the creator of the world and the Father of Jesus Christ.

God created the world and endowed Adam and Eve with freedom. It is precisely when freedom is rightly understood that history becomes significant. Plato had one republic; Augustine has two cities. The difference is their understanding of the cause of history. In Greek and Roman thought fate caused history, and history was correspondingly uninteresting at best, and at worst unintelligible. For Christians free choice—God's and man's—caused history, and history was the locus of salvation and hence a crucial and fascinating category. The Christians were the first to reflect at length on free choice and freedom.

For Irenaeus, creation and redemption are both part of one historical process, guided by divine providence and really affected by man's free choices—beginning with Adam's sin. Irenaeus, unlike Augustine, thinks of Adam and Eve as children and of their sin as a childish mistake. God gradually educates the human race and guides it through four covenants: in Adam, Noah, Moses, and the Gospel.[42] Christ is the second Adam. Here Irenaeus employs his important term "recapitulation." It means, not "summing up," but "being a new head." Adam was the first head of the human race, and sinned. Christ is the second, new head, and he got it all right. But still, continuity outweighs discontinuity. The basic pattern of providence and freedom remains, and Christ is a completion rather than a reversal.

Irenaeus fits his understanding of the Old Testament into this pattern. In the fourth book of *Against the Heresies,* Irenaeus wrote this important sentence: "They [the Jews] had a law, a discipline, and a prophecy of future things."[43] By "law" Irenaeus means

---

[42] *Against the Heresies* 3, 11, 8 (SC 211, 168–170). In *Against the Heresies* 3, 12, 11 (SC 211, 230), he writes that the words of the Old Testament are "fitted for their times."

[43] Ibid., 4, 15, 1 (SC 100, 548): "Itaque lex et disciplina erat illis et prophetia futurorum."

primarily the Ten Commandments, which remain in force for Christians. The "discipline" is primarily the cultic and ritual laws, which Christians did not observe. "Prophecy" is the typology found in the Old Testament. So far, Irenaeus does not differ radically from his Christian predecessors. What makes him distinctive is his insistence that all three aspects—law, discipline, and prophecy—were ordered by God both for the sake of Israel and for the Christian dispensation. "Law" and "prophecy" are easily understood; "discipline" is more difficult. Irenaeus thinks of "discipline," the cultic and ritual laws, as God's way of educating the human race as it grew from Adam's childishness to maturity; these laws "educated the soul through external and corporeal objects and drew it, as if by a chain, to obey the commandments, so that man might learn to obey God."[44] Thus, for Irenaeus, the Jewish Scriptures become the necessary preparation for the New Covenant; and the important word is "necessary." The history of Israel is a part of the total story of humanity's growth from childhood to perfection.

Conclusions

Irenaeus set the course for the Church's stance toward the Old Testament: it reveals the working of God's providential plan for the human race, but Jesus the Christ is the key to its interpretation. But this stance is not without problems and a certain ambiguity.

It is painful to say to others, "We take your Scriptures as our own, because we have the key that unlocks their meaning"; yet I do not know how Christians can say otherwise.

There also remains an ambiguity in Christians' use of their Old Testament. The liturgy is always a good test of doctrine. We Catholics read the Old Testament at Mass each Sunday, except during the fifty days from Easter to Pentecost, and conclude the reading by saying "Word of the Lord," just as we do when St. Paul, or other New Testament letters, are read. But the Old Testament reading is chosen to complement the gospel reading. On the one hand, we may say—rightly—that the Old Testament is no less the word of the Lord than the New Testament is. On the other hand, the

---

[44] Ibid., 4, 13, 2 (SC 100, 528).

Old Testament is somehow subordinated to the proclamation of Christ, to the first and oldest Christian creed, "Jesus is Lord."

In the final analysis, that ambiguity may not be a bad thing. St. Paul reminds us that "for now we see through a glass, darkly" (1 Cor 13:12). St. Augustine could write that the Scriptures themselves are transitory: "In the presence of such a day [when Christ shall come], lamps will not be needed: no prophet shall then be read to us, no book of an apostle shall be opened; we shall not require the witness of John, we shall not need the Gospel itself. Accordingly all Scriptures shall be taken out of the way—which, in the night of this world, were as lamps kindled for us that we might not remain in darkness."[45] We live now by faith, and may not claim to understand God's providential plan fully. Only when the fullness of grace is manifested will God give us complete understanding; to him, Father, Son, and Holy Spirit, be praise and glory now and forever.

---

[45] Augustine, *Tractates on the Gospel of John* 35, 9, trans. John Gibb and James Innes; NPNF, 1st series, 7 (orig. publ. 1888; repr. Grand Rapids: Eerdmans, 1974) 207.

3 Living Lord or Steadfast Word?

The Emergence of the New Testament

Three passages from early Christian writings will serve as a framework for understanding the emergence of the New Testament. At the end of St. Matthew's Gospel, Jesus says to his disciples:

> All authority in heaven and on earth has been given to me. Go therefore and make disciples of all nations, baptizing them in the name of the Father and of the Son and of the Holy Spirit, teaching them to observe all that I have commanded you (Matt 28:18-20).

Jesus thus gives the Eleven four commands: "go," "make disciples," "baptize," and "teach." Neither here nor anywhere else does he ever say: "write books."

Around the year 140, an interesting man named Papias of Hierapolis in Asia Minor reminisced about his days as a young Christian and wrote:

> But if by chance anyone came who had followed the elders, I inquired about the words of the elders: what Andrew or Peter said, or what Philip, or Thomas or James, or John or Matthew or any other of the Lord's disciples, or what Aristion and the elder John, the Lord's disciples, said. For I did not suppose that things from books would help me as much as things from a living and surviving voice.[1]

---

[1] Prologue to *Exegesis of the Lord's Oracles,* preserved by Eusebius, *Ecclesiastical History* 3, 39, 4; trans. Robert M. Grant, *Second-Century Christianity: A Collection of Fragments* (London: SPCK, 1957) 65–66.

Papias preferred a living voice to "things from books," as he disparagingly calls them—and those books were soon to be part of the New Testament.

Forty or fifty years later, between 180 and 190, Irenaeus of Lyons wrote:

> The gospels cannot be more in number, or fewer, than they are. For there are four zones of the world in which we live, and four principal winds; and the Church is spread over all the earth, and the pillar and foundation of the Church is the Gospel and the Spirit of life; so it fittingly has four pillars. . . .[2]

A great shift has taken place. Irenaeus not only defends books and those "things from books" that Papias disparaged, but he also has a precise list of authoritative books—four Gospels, no more and no fewer. In other words, he has a New Testament canon. His faith is in the living Lord, but he finds that Lord in the steadfast word of Scripture. The contrast between Papias and Irenaeus, separated by only forty or fifty years, epitomizes the topic: "Living Lord or Steadfast Word?" or, how the New Testament emerged.

The Shape of the New Testament

All Christians appeal to a New Testament as God's word. That New Testament is a collection of twenty-seven books. They vary greatly in length. The longest is the Gospel according to Luke, forty-six pages in the Revised Standard Version; the shortest is the Second Epistle of John, only thirteen verses.

Most of the books of the New Testament were written in the second half of the first century, that is, between A.D. 50 and 100. A few short books may be later. St. Paul's letters are the earliest group: they were written between 50 and 60. The Gospels took on their final shape between 70 and 100. Luke wrote the Acts of the Apostles around the time he wrote the Gospel. John the Presbyter wrote the Apocalypse toward the end of the first century. The Epistle to the Hebrews dates from about the same time. And with that, we have the bulk of the New Testament writings.

---

[2] Irenaeus, *Against the Heresies* 3, 11, 8 (SC 211, 160–162), trans. Cyril C. Richardson et al., *Early Christian Fathers,* LCC (Philadelphia: Westminster, 1953) 382 (altered).

The twenty-seven books fall into several clear groups. There are four Gospels—or rather one Gospel according to four authors, Matthew, Mark, Luke, and John, the "fourfold Gospel," as Irenaeus called it.[3] Thirteen letters bear St. Paul's name. Another book, the Epistle to the Hebrews, came to be thought of as Paul's, so that the final corpus of Pauline letters is fourteen books. There are also seven catholic epistles, called "catholic" because they are addressed not to single churches but to all Christians. One is from James, two from Peter; three are called Letters of John, although they do not have John's name in them; and one is from Jude. Six of the seven are attributed to Jesus' three closest disciples: Peter, James, and John. There are also two "stray" books: the Acts of the Apostles, by the author of Luke's gospel, and the Apocalypse, by John the Presbyter.

In ancient symbolism, the number four stood for the world, and four Gospels stand for universality. Seven was the number of perfection. There are seven catholic epistles, and twice seven Pauline letters. The Apocalypse contains seven letters to seven churches.

The Christian New Testament parallels the Jewish Scriptures in its structure. The Jewish Scriptures have three parts: the Law, the Prophets, and the Writings. The New Testament has not three parts, but two: the "Gospel" and the "Apostle." It is like a binary star system, in which two stars revolve around each other, with each star having its system of planets. The "Gospel" is the four written Gospels. The Acts of the Apostles and the Apocalypse of John, as the work of Luke and John, revolve around the Gospel like giant planets. The "Apostle," interestingly, is St. Paul, who was never a disciple of Jesus. The Epistle to the Hebrews was drawn into the Pauline sun, and the catholic epistles are seven little planets that revolve around that sun.

There is virtually no disagreement among Christians on which books belong to the New Testament. In the Middle Ages in the West, a short Pauline letter called the *Epistle to the Laodicenes* lurked around the edges of the canon, but never gained permanent admittance. Martin Luther put Hebrews, James, Jude, and the Apocalypse at the end of his German New Testament, and so disliked the Letter of James that he called it "an epistle of straw," but he never eliminated these books from the New Testament.

---

[3] Ibid., 3, 11, 8 (SC 211, 162, 168).

So the shape of the New Testament is easily seen; its origins, however, are not so easily explained. The topic can be complex, and it helps to keep a basic chronology in mind. In A.D. 30, which is probably the date of the first Easter, there was no New Testament. That is not at all surprising. A hundred years later, in 130, there was still no New Testament. That could be quite surprising. Rather suddenly, about 180, there is a New Testament. That bears further investigation. The New Testament appears for the first time, but in full clarity, in Irenaeus's work *Against the Heresies*. Irenaeus has a closed canon of four Gospels.[4] His canon of Pauline letters is not closed, but he puts Paul's letters on the same level as the Gospels.[5] He calls Acts "Scripture,"[6] and has two apocalypses in his canon of Scripture: the Apocalypse of John and the *Shepherd* of Hermas.[7] He may be the first to use the title "New Testament" of a collection of books.[8] An important ratio also shifts. Christian writers before Irenaeus cited the Old Testament relatively often, and quoted the Christian books that would later comprise the New Testament only rarely, if at all. Irenaeus, in contrast, cites New Testament writings twice as often as he cites the Old Testament: the Old Testament about five hundred times, the New more than one thousand times.[9]

By the year 200 most of the Christian Church possessed a common New Testament consisting of twenty books: four Gospels,

[4] Ibid., 3, 11, 8 (SC 211, 160–162).

[5] "Wherefore also Marcion and his followers have set themselves to mutilating the Scriptures, wholly rejecting some books and mutilating the Gospel according to Luke and the Epistles of Paul . . ." (*Against the Heresies,* 3, 12, 12 [SC 211, 232]).

[6] *Against the Heresies* 3, 12, 9 (SC 211, 222–224).

[7] For the Apocalypse see, for example, *Against the Heresies* 5, 35, 2 (SC 153, 444–448). On the *Shepherd* see ibid., 4, 20, 2 (SC 100, 628). See also ibid., 3, 3, 3 (SC 211, 34–36) on *First Clement*.

[8] *Against the Heresies* 4, 9, 1 (SC 100, 478), although the assertion is disputed.

[9] "In his *Adversus Haereses* he quotes 1,075 passages from almost all of the books of the New Testament: 626 from the Gospels, 54 from Acts, 280 from the Pauline Epistles (but not from Philemon), 15 from the Catholic Epistles (but not 2 Pet, 3 John, or Jude), and 29 from the Book of Revelation" (Bruce M. Metzger, *The Canon of the New Testament: Its Origin, Development, and Significance* [Oxford: Clarendon, 1987] 154).

thirteen Pauline letters, the Acts of the Apostles, the First Epistle of Peter, and the First Epistle of John. The now-standard New Testament of twenty-seven books was not fixed until about the year 400.

What concerns us here, though, is not the final shape of the New Testament, but a far more important question: why was there a New Testament at all? The crucial period is the one between 30 and 180. The idea of a New Testament emerged only toward the end of this 150-year period. So the Church survived its first century and a half without a New Testament. Why did a New Testament emerge? Why this one? What criteria were used to make that decision? The New Testament is the cornerstone of the Christian Church, and any question about its origin is a crucial one.

The New Testament is one answer to the question, What is the authority for Christian truth? There is only one unconditioned or absolute authority for Christian truth: namely, the Lord—Jesus of Nazareth, who died for our sins, and whom God raised up from the dead and made Messiah and Lord.[10] Christ is the final authority essentially because of who he was and what he did, because of his person and his deed in the Easter mystery; and then, because of that, for what he said and taught.

From the first day of its existence, Christianity also had a Bible, authoritative Scriptures: that is, the Jewish Scriptures interpreted through Christ.

When we look for a New Testament, we can set our sights this way: a New Testament exists when a collection of Christian writings is generally accepted in the Church as equal in authority to the Jewish Scriptures that the Church had already made its own. Put simply, there is a New Testament when the Church acknowledges "Volume II" of the Bible.

The search for the origins of the New Testament is made more difficult by the fact that the first half of the second century is the most obscure period in the entire history of the Church. As the first century drew to a close, the Church was still in biblical times. Peter and Paul had been dead for only thirty years. Wandering missionaries were founding new churches. The books that would make up the New Testament were still being written. Around 150, in contrast, the Church emerges from the shadows in a form that is

[10] See 1 Cor 15:3-5; Acts 2:36.

easily recognized. The leader of each local Church is a bishop, who has a council of presbyters or elders as advisers, and some deacons to assist him. Baptism is a rite of initiation that follows an extended period of instruction and testing. The Eucharist is celebrated each Sunday. Norms for continuing membership in the Church, and for dealing with serious, public sinners, are established. Frequent contact between Churches leads toward uniformity of practice. The Church has taken on the essential contours that still define its organization.

Exploring the period from 100 to 150 is like trying to find your way through a town, not only before there are any street signs, but before there are any streets. You see a few trees, some piles of earth being moved around by bulldozers, and some stakes with bright orange tape tied to them. You can perhaps picture where the main street will be, how side streets will branch off, and maybe where trees are being left for a park. But still, it takes a lot of imagination.

The trees, the piles of earth, and the stakes are the writings of authors called the ''Apostolic Fathers.'' We have about ten documents from the first half of the second century. Most of them are short, occasional writings. None of their authors qualifies as a theologian and, in one case at least (Hermas, who wrote the *Shepherd*), the author may not have been too bright. But they are all we have, and we have to make do with them.

I will consider each of the two main parts of the New Testament, the Gospel and the Apostle, under two topics: authority and collection.

The Gospels: The Authority of the Lord and a Collection of Gospels

Between the first Easter and Irenaeus, we can distinguish three stages in the development of the Gospels: oral tradition, the composition of the Gospels, and the acceptance of the four Gospels as Scripture.

The first stage is oral tradition, or the handing-on of the Gospel by speaking and listening. Before anyone tried to write down what the Church proclaimed about Jesus, what he said and did was precisely *proclaimed*—that is, told and retold by apostles, prophets, and teachers, both to potential converts and to believing Christians at

Sunday worship. Precisely because it was oral, we have no written record of it. But such a stage must have existed, and for several decades, at least, the authority of the Lord resided in oral tradition.

At this stage it is necessary, and useful, to distinguish the words of Jesus from the "gospel," because "gospel" does not mean "written document" until around 150.[11] Ignatius of Antioch defines the content of "gospel": "But there is something special about the gospel—I mean the coming of the Savior, our Lord Jesus Christ, his Passion and resurrection."[12] He also anticipates the distinction of Old and New Testaments when he contrasts the prophets, or the prophets and the law, with the Gospel.[13]

At some point, Christians began to write down what was being proclaimed about Jesus. The four Gospels found in the New Testament received their final form between the years 70 and 100. But they are neither the only written Gospel documents nor the oldest. Luke's Gospel begins with the statement that "many have undertaken to compile a narrative about the things which have been accomplished among us" (Luke 1:1). Both Matthew and Luke used other, written sources for their Gospels: at least Mark and one other source. Moreover, the process of writing gospels did not stop with the familiar four. Many other gospels were written, some of them in the earlier part of the second century: the *Gospel of Thomas,* the *Gospel of the Egyptians,* and the *Gospel of the Hebrews* are among them. Such gospels fall into three classes. A few of them, like the *Gospel of Thomas,* may be sincere attempts to record things that Jesus said

---

[11] "Gospel" may mean a written document at one or two places in the *Didache,* but the first indisputable use is Justin's in *First Apology,* 66, 3, where he equates "memoirs of the apostles" with Gospels. This passage is also the earliest in which the word "gospel" is used in the plural.

[12] *Philadelphians* 9, 2 (trans. Richardson, 111).

[13] Ignatius does so in four places: *Philadelphians* 5, 2 (trans. Richardson, 109): "and the 'Prophets,' let us love them too, because they anticipated the gospel in their preaching"; ibid., 9, 2 (trans. Richardson, 111): "the beloved prophets announced his coming; but the gospel is the crowning achievement forever;" *Smyrnaeans* 5, 1 (trans. Richardson, 114): "the prophets and the law of Moses have failed to convince them,—nay, to this very day the gospel and the sufferings of each one of us have also failed"; and ibid. 7, 2 (trans. Richardson, 114): "Rather pay attention to the prophets and above all to the gospel. There we get a clear picture of the Passion and see that the resurrection has really happened."

or did. Others are gospels produced by fringe groups in the Christian movement, such as Ebionite Jewish-Christians, or Gnostics, to justify their own beliefs. A third group is best classified as fiction, like the *Infancy Gospel of James,* which is a pious novella about the childhood of Mary, the mother of Jesus.

To say that the Gospels were written is not to say that they immediately replaced the oral tradition as authoritative. Christians probably preferred the oral tradition for decades after written gospels were available, and some undoubtedly grumbled about "changes in the Church" around the year 150 when written gospels began to come into use. When Papias wrote "For I did not suppose that things from books would help me as much as things from a living and surviving voice," he may have anticipated the Catholic Traditionalist Movement.

In the period of the Apostolic Fathers, it is still the words of Jesus, rather than any written gospel, that are authoritative. When the Apostolic Fathers quote the Scriptures (and not all of them do), they almost invariably mean the Old Testament. They do not have a New Testament. But they quote the words of Jesus as authoritative seventeen times. A few passages will show an important pattern evolving.

In a few cases the Apostolic Fathers quote one of the Gospels verbatim. Polycarp of Smyrna writes: ". . . even as the Lord said, 'The spirit indeed is willing, but the flesh is weak,' "[14] quoting Matthew 26:41 exactly. The sermon called *Second Clement* reads: "The Lord says: 'No servant can serve two masters,' "[15] quoting Luke 16:13 exactly. The *Didache,* a short, fascinating manual on how to keep order in a church, has this: "You must not let anyone eat or drink of your Eucharist except those baptized in the Lord's name. For in reference to this the Lord said, 'Do not give what is sacred to dogs,' "[16] quoting Matthew 7:6, but applying it to the Eucharist—one of the earliest instances of the spiritual interpretation of a New Testament text.

In other cases words of Jesus are quoted that sound vaguely familiar, as if they were from one of the known Gospels, but in fact

[14] *Letter of Polycarp* 7, 2 = Matt 26:41 = Mark 14:38 (trans. Richardson, 134).

[15] *Second Clement* 6, 1 = Luke 16:13 (trans. Richardson, 195).

[16] *Didache* 9, 5 = Matt 7:6 (trans. Richardson, 175).

they are not. A good example is from the *First Epistle of Clement,* written in Rome around A.D. 96:

> Especially let us recall the words of the Lord Jesus, which he uttered to teach considerateness and patience. For this is what he said: "Show mercy, that you may be shown mercy. Forgive, that you may be forgiven. As you behave to others, so they will behave to you. As you give, so will you get. As you judge, so will you be judged. As you show kindness, so will you receive kindness. The measure you give will be the measure you get."[17]

Although the words may sound familiar, no single sentence in the passage is an exact quotation from the New Testament.

About half of the seventeen sayings of Jesus in the Apostolic Fathers are of this sort, showing that the words of Jesus were not yet in a fixed form.

The third type is quotations of Jesus' words that have little or no contact with the four Gospels. In the so-called *Epistle of Barnabas* we read: "And the Lord says: 'Behold, I make the last things like the first,' "[18] and "In such a way, he says, 'Those who desire to see me and to take hold of my kingdom ought to take me through affliction and suffering.' "[19] The author of *Second Clement* writes: "For when someone asked the Lord when his Kingdom was going to come, he said, 'When the two shall be one, and the outside like the inside, and the male with the female, neither male nor female.' "[20] Clement of Alexandria identifies the *Gospel of the Egyptians* as the source of this passage. The author of *Second Clement* also writes:

> For the Lord said, "You will be like lambs among wolves." But Peter replied by saying, "What if the wolves tear the lambs to

---

[17] *First Clement* 13, 2 (trans. Richardson, 49).

[18] *Epistle of Barnabas* 6, 13 (trans. Robert A. Kraft in *The Apostolic Fathers,* ed. Jack Sparks [Nashville and New York: Thomas Nelson, 1978] 278).

[19] Ibid., 7, 11 (trans. Kraft, 281 [altered]).

[20] *Second Clement* 12, 2 (trans. Richardson, 198). Clement of Alexandria (*Stromateis* 3, 92–93) quotes another version of this saying as Jesus' words to Salome from the *Gospel of the Egyptians*: "When you have trampled on the garment of shame and when the two become one and the male with the female [is] neither male nor female" (trans. in E. Hennecke and W. Schneemelcher, *New Testament Apocrypha,* vol. I, *Gospels and Related Writings,* ed. R. McL. Wilson

pieces?'' Jesus said to Peter: ''After their death the lambs should not fear the wolves, nor should you fear those who kill you and can do nothing more to you. But fear him who, when you are dead, has power over soul and body to cast them into the flames of hell.''[21]

What we see here, in other words, is the oral tradition beginning to go to seed. So far, the growth is not noxious, and the Apostolic Fathers do not attribute any words to Jesus that contradict the essence of the Christian Gospel. At worst, we read silly things like Jesus' saying, ''After their deaths the lambs should not fear the wolves.''

In the middle third of the second century, new signs begin to appear. We see more of those wooden stakes with orange tape tied to them, and the layout of the city becomes a little clearer.

A passage in the *Letter of Polycarp* (written ca. 135) is the oldest witness to a dispute about the meaning of Jesus' words. Polycarp writes: ''Whosoever perverts the sayings of the Lord to suit his own lusts and says there is neither resurrection nor judgment—such a one is the first-born of Satan.''[22]

Another important landmark is a Christian teacher named Justin the Philosopher and Martyr,[23] who died for the faith in A.D. 165. Justin came to Christianity as a result of his search for the true philosophy, and probably thought of Christianity as the truest and best philosophy. In his extant writings, Justin cites the words of Jesus about sixty times. He often speaks of the ''memoirs'' of the apostles,[24] which he identifies as ''gospels.''[25] Justin is the first Christian to use the word ''gospel'' in the plural; its meaning is shifting from ''the Christian proclamation'' to ''written accounts of that proclamation.'' There is also a good chance that Justin took the Gospels of Matthew, Mark, and Luke, selected and arranged some

---

[London: SCM, 1963] 168). There is a complete translation of Book 3 of the *Stromateis* in *Alexandrian Christianity,* trans. John E. L. Oulton and Henry Chadwick, LCC (Philadelphia: Westminster, 1954) 40–92.

[21] *Second Clement* 5, 2–4 (trans. Richardson, 195).

[22] *Letter of Polycarp* 7, 1 (trans. Richardson, 134).

[23] So called by Tertullian, in *Against the Valentinians* 5.

[24] Twice in the *First Apology,* 13 times in the *Dialogue with Trypho.*

[25] *First Apology* 66, 3.

sayings of Jesus' from them, and made a booklet of texts to distribute to his classes.

Another mid-century landmark is Marcion, the famous shipping magnate and heretic. Marcion established the first known canon of the New Testament. When he discarded the Old Testament, he did not leave his Church without Scriptures. Marcion believed that Paul was the only apostle who had understood the Gospel; so he constituted a Christian canon that contained ten letters of Paul and the Gospel according to Luke. But Marcion also thought that Judaizers had corrupted these writings, and proceeded to remove from them all positive references to Jews and to the Old Testament.

The course was set, and things moved quickly. The number of claims to possess the authentic words of Jesus was growing rapidly, and the content of those sayings was growing increasingly divergent. The need for a fixed—that is, written—authority was pressing. According to Justin, the "memoirs of the apostles or the writings of the prophets" were also read at the liturgy on Sunday, and were the subject of a sermon;[26] this practice, too, fostered the move toward a fixed, written collection.

With Irenaeus, we see the result: by 180, a collection of four Gospels is accepted, along with the Old Testament, as the normative Scriptures for Christians.

Thus the authority of the Gospels: a move from Jesus' words, remembered and repeated orally, to the authority of his words found in written documents, to accepting four written Gospels, and only four, as Scripture.

The other important topic is the four Gospels precisely as a collection. In the history of the canon, nothing is simple and nothing is obvious. Why four Gospels? The authors of the four Gospels give no indication that they mean their Gospels to be used in combination with other Gospels; Luke even writes that he intends to replace earlier, less complete accounts (Luke 1:1-4). The four Gospels are a problem because they sometimes differ, and in a few cases contradict each other. Pagans who read the Gospels were confused by them, and ocasionally mocked the Christians for being unclear even about their own founder.

An easy solution was available: use only one Gospel. Marcion took it, and used only Luke's Gospel. In Syria, a man named Ta-

---

[26] Ibid., 67 (trans. Richardson, 287).

tian took it, too: not by rejecting three Gospels, but by combining all four into one continuous narrative. He used John's Gospel as the framework and pieced Matthew, Mark, and Luke into it. For at least two centuries, the Christian Church in Syria read this book, called the *Diatessaron,* in its worship.

Modern theologians have also speculated on the significance of the fact that the Church reads not one Gospel, but four. Some have seen in this fact a biblical grounding for the existence of different denominations in Christendom, as if Matthew, Mark, Luke, and John somehow corresponded to Catholics, Baptists, Methodists, and Lutherans.[27] Others have seen in the four Gospels a biblical warrant for pluralism in theology. But neither denominational differences nor pluralism in theology were the intention of the early Church. Early Christians treated the fact of four Gospels as a bit of a problem, and solved the problem by explaining that all four proclaimed the same essential message. A fascinating document, called the *Muratorian Fragment,* which dates from about 180, puts this solution about as succinctly as could be done:

> And therefore, though various ideas are taught in the several books of the Gospels, yet it makes no difference to the faith of believers, since by one sovereign Spirit all things are declared in all of them concerning the Nativity, the Passion, the Resurrection, the conversation with his disciples and his two comings, the first in lowliness and contempt, which has come to pass, the second glorious and with royal power, which is to come.[28]

The Apostle:
A Collection of Letters and Their Authority

The case of the second major division of the New Testament, the Apostle, is different from—even the opposite of—the Gospels. Each of the Gospels was meant to be the complete story about

[27] See Gerhard Ebeling, "The New Testament and the Multiplicity of Confessions," in *The Word of God and Tradition: Historical Studies Interpreting the Divisions of Christianity,* trans. S. H. Hook (Philadelphia: Fortress, 1968) 148–159; and Ernst Käsemann, "The Canon of the New Testament and the Unity of the Church," in *Essays on New Testament Themes,* trans. W. J. Montague, Studies in Biblical Theology, 41 (Naperville: Allenson, 1964) 95–107.

[28] Cited from J. Stevenson, ed., *A New Eusebius: Documents Illustrative of the History of the Church to A.D. 337* (London: SPCK, 1968) 145.

Jesus. In assembling a collection of four Gospels, the Church's problem was to make the universal particular. In the case of Paul's letters, the problem was the opposite: to make the particular universal. For example, Paul wrote to the Christian Church at Corinth in the mid 50s to answer some questions and solve some problems. It is anything but obvious that what he wrote to Corinth should apply to other Christian communities, or, all the more, to all Christians for all time. Yet this is what happened.

Scholars have elaborated some fairly complex explanations of how Paul's letters were collected.[29] For example, one theory holds that Paul's letters were read and forgotten but, after Luke published the Acts of the Apostles, someone got interested in Paul, went around and collected his letters, and wrote Ephesians as a preface or summary. Another theory holds that, with the rise of Gnosticism, an unknown individual collected Paul's letters and rearranged them into a corpus of seven letters, anti-Gnostic in substance and catholic in shape. A third theory holds that a Pauline school preserved and edited Paul's authentic letters, wrote six new ones, and published the whole corpus.

It is unlikely that one individual is responsible for the collection of Paul's letters. Nor do they constitute one massive anti-Gnostic blast. That some editing has taken place, and that there are post-Pauline elements in the letters, is clear, although perhaps not so clear as some scholars assume.

To understand why Paul's letters were collected and circulated, it helps to ask how big a Christian library was in the year 50, or 100. The answer is: very, very small. In 50 it probably contained only the Old Testament. By 100 it could have contained some few Christian writings, too. And why did Christians need a library? For two principal reasons: to solve their problems and to help structure their worship.

The problems that Christian communities faced in A.D. 100 were mostly practical ones: how to organize and run a Church, how to establish norms for membership, how to conduct worship each week, how to regulate behavior. In 96, there had been a revolt in Corinth against the older clergy, who were thrown out of office. Bishop Ignatius of Antioch clearly had problems with Chris-

[29] This summary follows Harry Y. Gamble, *The New Testament Canon: Its Making and Meaning* (Philadelphia: Fortress, 1985) 36–41.

tians who resisted his authority. Defection was not unknown; a letter written around 117 by Pliny, a Roman governor in Asia Minor, shows us that some who had once been Christians had left the Church twenty years before—defections from the Church are not only a modern problem. In the first half of the second century, the best-known of Paul's letters was 1 Corinthians, precisely because it solved some specific problems about the organization of a Church.

The practice that shaped the early Christian Church more than any other was the weekly Eucharist. Christians met each week, on Sunday, sometimes twice. Anyone who has ever organized even one meeting knows the problems involved. If the worship, teaching, and fellowship ceased to be attractive or interesting, the community would dwindle or die out. The offering of the Eucharist was the heart of the worship, but preaching and exhortation were another important part. Paul's letters were surely first read to the community at its Sunday Eucharist. And when a community needed guidance, they could be read again.

The earliest Christians were undoubtedly eager to get whatever good Christian writings they could for guidance and for use in worship. The Christians at Rome had a copy of 1 Corinthians by the year 96.[30] Within a year of his writing them, Polycarp had a collection of Ignatius's letters;[31] he also had a copy of *First Clement*.[32] The author of 2 Peter knew a collection of Paul's letters.[33] The further, technical questions of the content and order of the collections need not concern us here. But, once they were collected, and especially once they were thought of as seven in number,[34] the number of completion, Paul's letters could be understood as God's word to his Church, precisely because they were the words of an apostle, one commissioned by Christ to proclaim the Gospel.

---

[30] The author of *First Clement* writes to the Corinthians: "Pick up the letter of the blessed apostle Paul. What was the primary thing he wrote to you . . .?" *First Clement* 47, 1–2 (trans. Richardson, 65).

[31] See *Letter of Polycarp* 13, 2.

[32] In 2, 3 he cites a version of the synoptic-type sayings found in *First Clement* 13, 2.

[33] See 2 Pet 4:16.

[34] As they are, for example, in the Muratorian Fragment.

Thus the collection of Paul's letters. Their authority can be treated more briefly. The "apostles" were the authoritative witnesses to Christ's resurrection. The office was not uncontroverted, and Paul, always ready for a fight, mentions the existence of "false apostles."[35] With the passing of time, the "apostles" were idealized. Ignatius of Antioch writes that the Lord acted through the apostles,[36] but also that the apostles enjoyed authority on their own. "I do not give you orders like Peter and Paul," he writes to the Christians at Rome; "they were apostles; I am a convict."[37] He even puts the apostles' authority on the same level as the Lord's.[38] Polycarp reveres the apostles because they "preached the gospel to us."[39] After the apostles had died, their authority passed rather naturally from their persons to their writings, because that was all the Church had left of them—that and a few tombs. Again, there were two steps. The first was: this letter is authoritative because an apostle, usually Paul, wrote it. The second was: this letter is authoritative, so an apostle must have written it. The best-known example of the latter is the Epistle to the Hebrews, which came to be thought of as Paul's.

Eventually, the authority of the Gospels was also reinforced with apostolic authority, and the names of apostles, or apostles' disciples, were attached to the four anonymous gospels. Thus the tradition soon developed that Matthew was the work of the apostle Levi, Mark was written by Peter's disciple, Luke was written by Paul's disciple, and John was the work of the Beloved Disciple.

Thus the future is fixed: the New Testament will contain letters by apostles, and Paul is the chief among them.

The Criteria for Canonicity

At the beginning of this lecture, I posed some questions. Why did a New Testament emerge? Why this one? Who decided what books belong to it? What criteria were used to make that decision?

---

[35] 2 Cor 11:13: "For such men are false apostles, deceitful workmen, disguising themselves as apostles of Christ."

[36] *Magnesians* 7, 1.

[37] *Romans* 4, 3 (trans. Richardson, 104).

[38] "Make a real effort, then, to stand firmly by the orders of the Lord and the apostles"; *Magnesians* 13, 1 (trans. Richardson, 97).

[39] *Letter of Polycarp* 6, 3 (trans. Richardson, 134).

Two have been answered, in a modest way. A New Testament emerged because the authority for Christian truth had to be fixed in a standard, and universally accessible, form. This New Testament emerged because the Gospel and the Apostle were the primary authorities for Christian truth.

If one asks, who decided what books belong to it, the answer is, "the Church," understood as a collectivity and represented especially by the bishops.

The question of the criteria that governed the formation of the New Testament can only be touched upon in a few concluding words.

In 1840 the Italian librarian Ludovico Muratori published a text he had discovered in an eighth-century manuscript. The text is called after him, the "Muratorian Fragment." It is eighty-five lines long, written in barbaric Latin, and comprises the oldest extant list of New Testament books. It was written in Rome around 180, and is probably a private rather than an official list.[40]

The New Testament that the list presupposes includes all the books of the later New Testament except Hebrews, James, 1 and 2 Peter, and perhaps 3 John. It adds the Wisdom of Solomon and the *Apocalypse of Peter,* the latter with hesitation.

The fragment illustrates all sorts of interesting aspects of the formation of the New Testament canon.

The Gospels, for example: the author knows four Gospels, since he calls Luke's the third; the beginning of the fragment is missing. He accepts the apostolic authority of the Gospels, calling Luke Paul's expert.[41] Against heretics, he defends the Gospels as the work of eye-witnesses. Apparently the authority of John's Gospel was in doubt, since the author describes at length how it has the authority of all the apostles behind it and is the result of divine inspiration.

The author also knows the problem of having four Gospels. Ancient readers were bothered by the fact that the Gospels started their

---

[40] Albert C. Sundberg, "Canon Muratori: A Fourth-Century List," *Harvard Theological Review* 66 (1973) 1–41 attempted to date the fragment in the fourth century and place it in the East, but his arguments have not been widely accepted.

[41] Ascribing Luke's Gospel to Paul's authority became a commonplace; see Irenaeus, *Against the Heresies* 3, 1, 1 (SC 211, 24) and Tertullian, *Against Marcion* 4, 2.

stories at different points, and even gave two different genealogies for Jesus. Different groups found different solutions. Marcion rejected every Gospel except one, Luke's. Tatian combined the four into one running narrative, the *Diatessaron* (a Greek word for "musical harmony"). The author of the Muratorian Fragment takes the solution that became standard: there may be four Gospels, but their teaching is one. His proofs are two. The one Holy Spirit guided their writing.[42] And they all teach the one rule of faith: Christ's birth, passion, resurrection, "conversation with his disciples," and second coming; the passage has already been quoted. In other words: by the power of the Holy Spirit all four Gospels teach the same truth, and the whole truth. The author repeats the same idea later, when he comments on Paul's Letter to the Romans that "Christ is the rule of the Scriptures and moreover their principle."

When he gets to the epistles, the author has an ingenious explanation for their universality. Paul, after all, wrote to single Churches and addressed those Churches' problems. Why should his letters be authoritative for all Churches? Because, the author writes, both Paul and John (the latter in the Apocalypse) write to seven Churches, and seven symbolizes universality; hence they write to all the Churches. The later acceptance of seven catholic epistles probably follows the same principle.

Most interesting are the criteria for inclusion—for canonicity, we may as well say. One criterion is early date: the *Shepherd* of Hermas is written too late to be included. Another is liturgical use: the *Apocalypse of Peter* is doubtful, because some do not want to have it read in church. So too, the *Shepherd* of Hermas may not be read publicly. Another is apostolic authorship: all the books named are by apostles or the disciples of apostles (such as Mark or Luke) except the Wisdom of Solomon (whose place in the list is quite odd).

But ultimately, these criteria do not suffice. The author has two letters, one to the Laodicenes and one to the Alexandrians, that claim to be Paul's. They bear Paul's name, but they cannot be received. Why? Because they are not orthodox. How does the author know that they are not? By checking them against the rule of faith. Hence, an important principle emerges: the formation of

---

[42] "Uno et principali spiritu": cf. Ps 50:14 LXX. See Irenaeus, *Against the Heresies* 3, 17, 2 (SC 211, 330), who also applies Ps 50:14 to the Holy Spirit.

the canon was guided by the rule of faith, the norm of orthodox belief.

The "rule of faith" is a crucially important concept, and one that we will consider at length a little later. It is the principle that guided the beliefs of these early Christians as they sought to hear and proclaim the word of God, to whom, Father, Son, and Holy Spirit, be glory and honor now and forever.

4 Comely King or Snarling Dog?

The Struggle to Interpret the Bible

In his great work against the Gnostics, Irenaeus of Lyons wrote:

Such, then, is their system, which neither the prophets announced, nor the Lord taught, nor the apostles delivered, but
of which they boast that beyond all others they have a perfect
knowledge. They gather their views from other sources than the
Scriptures and, to use a common proverb, they strive to weave
ropes out of sand. They endeavor to adapt with an air of proba-
bility to their own peculiar assertions the parables of the Lord,
the sayings of the prophets, and the words of the apostles, in
order that their scheme may not seem altogether without support. In doing so, however, they disregard the order and the connection of the Scriptures and, so far as in them lies, dismember
and destroy the truth. By transferring passages, and dressing them
up anew, and making one thing out of another, they succeed
in deluding many through their wicked art in adapting the oracles
of the Lord to their opinions. Their manner of acting is just as
if one, when a beautiful image of a king has been constructed
by some skilful artist out of precious jewels, should then take
this likeness of the man all to pieces, should re-arrange the gems,
and so fit them together to make them into the form of a dog
or of a fox, and even that but poorly executed; and should then
maintain and declare that this was the beautiful image of the king
which the skilful artist constructed, pointing to the jewels which
had been so admirably fitted together by the first artist to form
the image of the king, but have been with bad effect transferred
by the latter one to the shape of a dog, and by thus exhibiting
the jewels, should deceive the ignorant who had no conception
what a king's form was like, and persuade them that that miser-

able likeness of the fox was, in fact, the beautiful image of the king.[1]

The Scriptures are a great store of jewels. The skillful artist, who is the right-believing interpreter, has arranged them into a splendid picture of a king. The Gnostics wreck the picture of the king and rearrange the jewels to make a picture of a snarling dog or a glaring fox. And, Irenaeus assures us, it is not even a good picture of a dog or a fox. As a final outrage, the Gnostics try to persuade simple believers that the snarling dog is really the comely king.

In other words: Irenaeus and the Gnostics disagree about how to interpret the Bible. Tertullian was tempted simply to give up; he wrote once, "arguments about Scripture achieve nothing but a stomachache or a headache."[2] But Irenaeus would not give up; nor, in fact, did Tertullian.

One explanation might be that the Gnostics quote the Bible out of context, which is easy to do. Someone might assert that the Bible says: "There is no God"; and indeed it does, for Psalm 14:1 reads: "The fool says in his heart, 'There is no God.' "[3] Or one might recall the Victorian preacher who delivered an impassioned sermon against a fashionable hair-style for women. He climaxed his tirade by saying, "God himself forbids this extravagance, for Holy Scripture says, 'Top knot, come down.' " Asked later where the Bible says this, he answered confidently, "Matthew 24:17." The verse reads: "Let him who is on the housetop not come down."

But the problem was not quoting out of context. The methods that Irenaeus and the Gnostics used to interpret the Bible were remarkably similar. Irenaeus appealed to the prophets, the Lord, and the apostles. So did the Gnostics, and Irenaeus admits it. In what, then, do they err? In two points, Irenaeus writes: "they gather their views from other sources" and "they disregard the order and the connection of the Scriptures." Yet the Gnostics could say the same of Irenaeus. What, then, is the difference between Irenaeus and the Gnostics? How can Irenaeus say that he is right,

---

[1] Irenaeus, *Against the Heresies* 1, 8, 1 (SC 264, 112–116), trans. Alexander Roberts and W. H. Rambaut, ANF 1 (repr. Grand Rapids: Eerdmans, 1973) 326 (altered).

[2] *On the Prescription of Heretics* 16.

[3] So also Ps 53:1.

and the Gnostics wrong? To understand the difference is the topic at hand, "The Struggle to Interpret the Bible."

I would like to begin with some ideas about ancient approaches to reading and education and go on to consider four different approaches to interpreting the Bible that were used in the early Church, or outside it.

Education, Reading, and Interpretation in Antiquity

To begin, I propose a simple thought: the way the Bible is read depends upon the way people are taught to read.

Greeks and Romans had national epics: Homer's *Iliad* and *Odyssey* for the Greeks, Vergil's *Aeneid* for the Romans. These epics were a sort of sacred text, and much of the culture was passed on in schools by the explanation—we could as well say the "exegesis"—of these epic poems. Teachers explained these sacred texts in one of the most uninspiring ways imaginable: word by word by word.

For the ancients, the first unit of understanding was not the complete narrative, or even the sentence, but the word. St. Augustine's dialogue *On the Teacher* illustrates this point superbly. When those trained in this way read the Bible, they changed the text they read but not the method they used to read. This fact explains a great deal about the approach that the Fathers of the Church took to the Scriptures. More than a few apparent obscurities in the Fathers' writings are clarified by realizing that they were using, explaining, or accounting for a single word from the Scriptures.

We have seen that Irenaeus thought of the Scriptures as a great mass of precious jewels, which had to be arranged into a mosaic. The great biblical scholar Origen thinks the same way, and also uses an intriguing image. In his *Commentary on the Psalms* he related a comparison that he heard from the rabbi who taught him Hebrew: the Scripture is like one great house that has many, many rooms. All the rooms are locked. At each locked door there is a key, but it is not the key to that door. The scholar's task is to match the keys to their doors; and this is a great labor.[4]

---

[4] On Psalm 1, in *Philocalia* 2, 3, ed. Marguérite Harl; SC 302 (Paris: Cerf, 1983) 245. See Joseph T. Lienhard, "Origen as Homilist," in *Preaching in the Patristic Age: Studies in Honor of Walter J. Burghardt, S.J.,* ed. David G. Hunter (New York/Mahwah: Paulist, 1989) 47–48.

Another difference lay in the skill that reading required. In ancient Greek and Latin writing, no space was left between words. The skill of reading was, first of all, the skill of discerning: of grouping the letters rightly, so that they formed intelligible words. Moreover, ancients read aloud, even when they read privately. In the Acts of the Apostles, Philip hears the Ethiopian eunuch reading the prophet Isaiah.[5] Augustine is amazed when he sees Ambrose reading and cannot hear anything.[6] In his *Rule,* Benedict allows his monks either to sleep or to read after dinner, but those who were reading were not to disturb the others.[7] Reading aloud profoundly affected the reader's relationship to a text; reading for the ancients was much closer to memorizing than it is for us. Evelyn Wood's speed reading was not only impossible, but unthinkable. To begin to appreciate St. Augustine's *Confessions,* for example, one should sit alone in a garden and read them aloud.

Just as pagan teachers explained their national epics, so Christian teachers explained the Bible. When the Fathers wrote about the Bible, they used three literary forms: scholia, commentaries, and homilies, which corresponded roughly to three settings: the reference room, the research library, and the pulpit.

Scholia are the equivalent of long footnotes. Origen began the process, and made sets of notes on large parts of the Bible. He explained the significance of place names, the meaning of Hebrew words, and so on. Most of his scholia are lost. Augustine did something similar. He took the first seven books of the Bible, the Letter to the Romans, and other books, and made notes on difficult passages. Quite possibly, these notes are the result of a group reading and discussion of the book in question with his friends or fellow clergy.

Commentaries are a distinct literary form. They are the product of the study or the library, and not of the pulpit. By its very nature a commentary attempts to say something about each significant word or phrase in a book. The more difficult or obscure the phrase, the more challenged the author is and the more time he spends on it. Commentaries could grow to enormous proportions. Origen wrote thirty-two books on St. John's Gospel and only finished half of it when he gave up.

---

[5] Acts 8:30.
[6] *Confessions* 6, 3, 3.
[7] *Rule of St. Benedict* 48, 5.

Homilies take a wholly different approach to Scripture.[8] The word "homily" itself meant "conversation" in a familiar group, but also "instruction," and could designate the instruction that a philosopher gave his pupils in familiar conversation. Christians used it to designate the simple, familiar explanation of the Scriptures given at the Eucharist, to distinguish that sort of speaking from the formal speech *(logos)* familiar from secular life. The homily was limited in time, since the congregation could not stand indefinitely (although Augustine's hearers sometimes stood for an hour, and Chrysostom's for two or three hours). It was also limited in subject matter, to the biblical passage that the lector or deacon had read (although in Origen's time, at least, a reading from the Old Testament might comprise two or three modern chapters). It was also limited by the audience, since it was supposed to make sense to the auditors (although, as someone remarked, Augustine spent a good deal of time explaining neoplatonism to farmers and stevedores). It was defined by its purpose, which was to show that the Scriptures said something worthwhile to the people about their lives. The art of preaching eventually drew the attention of a few Fathers.[9]

When the Fathers studied the Bible, they used the methods they had learned in their rhetorical education. But they also added something: namely, Christian faith. They believed that the Bible is the Word of God, inspired by the Holy Spirit. Since this is so, three things could be said about the whole Bible, and about any part of it: what the Holy Spirit says is never wrong; what the Holy Spirit says is never trite; and what the Holy Spirit says always speaks to me to enlighten and guide me.

In other words they assumed that the whole Bible, and all its parts, are true. And since this is the case, the whole Bible must contain a single, unified teaching. If it appears not to, then the problem is in our perception, not in the Bible itself. Moreover, biblical truth is always significant, even profound; and passages that

[8] For what follows, see Joseph T. Lienhard, "Homily," in *Encyclopedia of Early Christianity,* ed. Everett Ferguson et al. (New York and London: Garland, 1990) 531–533.

[9] John Chrysostom's book *On the Priesthood* contains a chapter on the office of preaching, and the fourth book of Augustine's *On Christian Doctrine* is the first Christian treatise on homiletics.

appear superficial must have a deeper meaning. And finally, the Bible, read rightly, will always speak to me and help me. The faith of the modern believer, hearing the Scriptures proclaimed in church or reading them meditatively, makes the same assumptions.

Gnostics' Methods of Interpretation

The originality of heretics is noteworthy. Marcion published the first known canon of the New Testament. The first known commentary on any New Testament book was written around the year 170 by a Valentinian Gnostic named Heracleon. He wrote a commentary on the Gospel according to John even before that book was securely in the New Testament.

When Heracleon came to study the Gospel according to John, he already knew a lot about the universe. He knew that spirit and matter were opposed to each other, and that matter was at best rather nasty, and at worst evil. In fact, matter and spirit were so sharply opposed that they could not come from a common source. An inferior craftsman (*demiurge*, in Greek) had made the material world. Besides the material world, there was a higher world of spirit, called the *pleroma*. Heracleon also knew that there are three kinds of human natures or human beings, which are determined and immutable. The three are spiritual souls, psychic or animal souls, and earthy souls. The spirituals had so strong an affinity for the world of spirit that they could not help but be saved. The earthy souls, because of their nature, had no chance of salvation. The psychic or animal souls could, like Avis, try harder.

Categories like matter and spirit, and the three kinds of souls, gave Heracleon his tools for interpreting the Bible.[10] Old and New Testaments, for example, fitted easily into matter and spirit. The God of the Old Testament, after all, had created the material world.[11] Christ, who, according to Heracleon, came from the spiritual pleroma and far outranked the Demiurge of the Old Testament, said in John 4:24 that God is spirit, and should be worshipped in spirit and in truth. To give only one more example: Jacob's well,

[10] Fragments of Heracleon's commentary are quoted from Robert M. Grant, *Second-Century Christianity: A Collection of Fragments* (London: SPCK, 1957) 39–52.

[11] Frag. 1; frag. 20: matter is evil; frag. 22: Jews worship the Demiurge.

mentioned in Jesus' conversation with the Samaritan woman in John 4:12, is a feeble, short-lived, deficient source of water because it is earthly, and Jacob was from the Old Testament. The spiritual water that the Savior will give (John 4:14) is eternal, incorruptible, and permanent.[12]

Everywhere Heracleon finds evidence of three sorts of human beings. When Jesus goes "down to Caphernaum" he descends to the level of matter and can do nothing there.[13] When he goes "up to Jerusalem," he advances from matter to *psyche* or *anima*.[14] The temple has three parts: the holy of holies is for the high priest, or spirituals; the court of the temple is for Levites, or psychics; and the place where oxen and sheep are sold is for mere merchants, the earthy clods who are lost. Jesus predicts his resurrection "in three days": the first day is the earthy day, the second the psychic day, and the third the spiritual day, on which the resurrection of the Church takes place.[15] Christ is the Logos or "Word"; John the Baptist is merely a voice (that is, "the voice of one crying in the wilderness"[16]); the Old Testament prophets are no more than sound.

Other examples of Gnostic exegesis abound. Valentinian Gnostics held a hierarchy of thirty celestial Aeons, and found the thirty Aeons "most plainly indicated"[17] in Jesus' parable of the workers in the vineyard:[18] for the owner sends out workers at the first, third, sixth, ninth, and eleventh hours and, totalled up, they make thirty.[19] They also took the five foolish virgins[20] to be the five bodily senses, silly and easily deceived, whereas the five wise virgins are the five intellectual faculties that attain mysterious, supernal truth.[21] Carpocrates used Jesus' words about "paying the last farthing" (Matt 5:26) to confirm his doctrine of reincarnation.[22] Tertullian,

---

[12] Frag. 17; John 4:14.
[13] Frag. 11; John 2:12.
[14] Frag. 13; John 2:14.
[15] Frag. 15; John 2:19 reading "in three days" instead of "on the third day."
[16] Matt 3:3, citing Isa 40:3.
[17] Irenaeus, *Against the Heresies* 1, 1, 3 (SC 264, 34).
[18] Matt 20:1-16.
[19] Irenaeus, *Against the Heresies* 1, 1, 3 (SC 264, 34).
[20] Matt 25:1-13.
[21] Tertullian, *On the Soul* 18, 4.
[22] Ibid., 35, 1.

who relates the story, protests: "Thus he distorts the meaning of that remark of our Lord which is perfectly clear and straightforward and should be understood in its obvious meaning."[23] Tertullian is hardly the last to appeal, a little naively, to the "obvious meaning."

The Church rejected Heracleon, along with other Gnostics, as heretics, and thereby affirmed its faith that there is one God, revealed both in the Old Testament and in Christ; that this one God made everything that exists, and all that he made is good; and that God offers salvation to every human being.

The Church might simply have reaffirmed its basic teachings and stopped there. But the Gnostics, strange as it seems, had a great appeal in the second century. They offered, in their own minds, a form of Christianity for intellectuals, for those who knew that the idea of a god who became man in time and died on a cross had to be a myth that stood for a deeper truth. Simply to reaffirm its beliefs put the Church at risk of anti-intellectualism, a risk it happily did not take. Two men stand out in their reaction to the Gnostics: Irenaeus and Origen. Irenaeus showed that the basic confession of historical Christianity, that the Son of God became man, died on the cross, and was raised up, was not a myth; it was the key to interpreting the Scriptures. Origen showed that a true intellectual could accept historical Christianity and give a wholly responsible account of his belief.

Irenaeus and the Rule of Faith

Irenaeus is a crucial figure in the history of Christianity. With Irenaeus, the last vestiges of primitive Christianity are gone. He is the first orthodox writer who clearly and obviously possesses a New Testament. He is also the first witness to a fierce dispute about the interpretation of the New Testament. In other words, no sooner did the Church acquire a New Testament than dispute about its meaning began.

Irenaeus has a clear answer to the problem the Gnostics posed. There is a guide to the right interpretation of the Scriptures. It is not the opposition of matter and spirit, or three kinds of souls.

---

[23] Ibid., 35, 2, trans. Edwin A. Quain, *Tertullian: Apologetical Works*, FC 10 (New York: Fathers of the Church, 1950) 263.

That guide is called the "rule of faith," which is a crucially important concept.

Irenaeus regularly appeals to the "rule of faith" as the norm for interpreting the Scriptures correctly. In several places in his writings, he gives a formulation of the "rule." Each time, the formulation is different, but the general pattern is easy to discern. It is this: the Church believes in one God, Father and creator; in Jesus the Christ, God's Son, who took flesh to save us; and in the Holy Spirit. In other words, the heart of the rule of faith is belief in one God who is Father, Son, and Spirit, and in the incarnation of the Son of God to deliver us from sin.

Two examples should illustrate what Irenaeus means by the rule of faith. In the first book of *Against the Heresies* he writes:

> The Church, though dispersed throughout the whole world, even to the ends of the earth, has received from the apostles and their disciples this faith: [She believes] in one God, the Father almighty, maker of heaven, and earth, and the sea, and all things that are in them; and in one Christ Jesus, the Son of God, who became incarnate for our salvation; and in the Holy Spirit, who proclaimed through the prophets the dispensations of God, and the advents, and birth from a virgin, and the passion, and the resurrection from the dead, and the ascension into heaven in the flesh of the beloved Christ Jesus, our Lord, and his [future] manifestation from heaven in the glory of the Father "to gather all things in one" (Eph 1:10), and to raise up anew all flesh of the whole human race. . . . As I have already observed, the Church, having received this preaching and this faith, although scattered throughout the whole world, yet, as if occupying but one house, carefully preserves it.[24]

And in the third book, he writes of

> . . . the ancient tradition, believing in one God, the Creator of heaven and earth, and all things therein, by means of Christ Jesus, the Son of God; who, because of His surpassing love towards His creation, condescended to be born of the virgin, He Himself uniting man through Himself to God, and having

---

[24] Irenaeus, *Against the Heresies* 1, 10, 1–2 (SC 264, 154–158), trans. Alexander Roberts, ANF 1, 330–331.

suffered under Pontius Pilate, and rising again, and having been received up in splendor, shall come in glory. . . .[25]

The rule is a rule of *faith*. Christianity stands out from other religions in its insistence on the importance of doctrine, which means "teaching." At the end of Matthew's Gospel, Jesus says to his disciples: "Go therefore and make disciples of all nations, . . . teaching them . . ." (Matt 28:19-20). Those who have been taught the faith confess what they believe. Paul writes: "If you confess with your lips that Jesus is Lord, and believe in your heart that God raised him from the dead, you will be saved" (Rom 10:9). "Jesus is Lord" is the first and oldest Christian creed. We read in the First Letter to Timothy: "The truth is this: God is one. One also is the mediator between God and men, the man Christ Jesus, who gave himself as a ransom for all" (1 Tim 2:4-6).

The rule of faith is also a *rule*. A rule is a norm against which something else is measured, like a ruler used to measure a piece of paper. The rule of faith may sound like a creed, but it is not the same as a creed. The rule of faith is invoked by theologians; creeds arose out of the sacrament of baptism. The rule is adequate for faith even without written documents, as Irenaeus writes: "For how should it be if the apostles themselves had not left us writings? Would it not be necessary to follow the course of the tradition which they handed down to those to whom they did commit the Churches?"[26]

The rule of faith is so central, Irenaeus writes, that those who cannot read can still have the rule imprinted on their hearts, and thereby preserve the orthodox faith. He writes: "To which course many nations of those barbarians who believe in Christ do assent, having salvation written in their hearts by the Spirit, without paper or ink, and, carefully preserving the ancient tradition, believing in one God. . . . Those who, in the absence of written documents, have believed this faith, are barbarians, so far as regards our language; but as regards doctrine, manner, and tenor of life, they are, because of faith, very wise indeed. . . ."[27]

---

[25] Ibid., 3, 4, 2 (SC 211, 46–48), trans. Roberts, ANF 1, 417. The one final norm (after Christ) that Irenaeus acknowledges, is the "rule of truth."

[26] Ibid., 3, 4, 1 (SC 211, 46), trans. Roberts, ANF 1, 417.

[27] Ibid., 3, 4, 2 (SC 211, 46–48), trans. Roberts, ANF 1, 417.

Thus one effect of what Irenaeus does is to relativize the New Testament. At first hearing that may sound like a bad thing to do. Perhaps it is better to put it this way: he shows that the New Testament, the whole Bible, stands in a particular relationship to God, Christ, the truth, the apostolic tradition, and the Church.

Thus Irenaeus's answer to the Gnostics. What enables Irenaeus to arrange all the jewels in the Bible into a mosaic of the comely king is the rule of faith; without the rule of faith, the biblical gems can be remade into the picture of anything one wishes, no matter how ugly, foul, or lowly.

Origen and Allegory

Origen is one of the most important theologians of the early Church and one of the most influential Christian writers of all time. He was born in 185 or 186 into a Christian family in Alexandria in Egypt.[28] When he was seventeen his father Leonides died as a martyr for the faith, and the young Origen became a teacher of grammar to support his mother and his six younger brothers and sisters. He also began to teach catechism—that is, to instruct pagans interested in Christianity. A few years later, probably when his brothers were able to support the family, Origen devoted himself to studying and teaching the Scriptures. He also began to live an intensely ascetical life.[29] In 232 he was ordained a priest in Caesarea in Palestine without the consent of the bishop of Alexandria, who then turned against him and caused him to leave Alexandria for Caesarea. Origen took his library and his assistants with him. He spent the last twenty years of his life in Caesarea, where he died in 254 or 255; his death was probably hastened by the torture he suffered in the persecution under the emperor Decius.

Origen was, heart and soul, a man of the Bible, a man who devoted his life to explaining God's Word. His mind was acute, his memory tenacious, his curiosity inexhaustible, and his patience unbreakable. He was a man who was most content when he could study, analyze, and comment on a biblical text. Origen even helped shape the New Testament: five or six of the shorter books of the New Testament are in the canon because of Origen's authority.

---

[28] For what follows see Lienhard, "Origen as Homilist."
[29] See Eusebius, *Ecclesiastical History* 6, 3.

From his study of the Bible, Origen developed a theological system. His theology was intellectually rigorous, but it did not stop there. It had a practical goal, for it was a system of mysticism, which would lead the believer to union with God.

Origen was controversial during his lifetime, and far more so after his death. Origenist and anti-Origenist parties criss-cross the landscape of ancient Church history. In 553, almost exactly three centuries after his death, the fifth ecumenical council condemned Origen as a heretic. G. L. Prestige has written touchingly: "Origen is the greatest of that happily small company of saints who, having lived and died in grace, suffered sentence of expulsion from the Church on earth after they had already entered into the joy of their Lord."[30] But wariness of Origen, and outright rejection of him as a man who merely adorned Platonic philosophy with a few Christian terms, continued well into the twentieth century, until the great Jesuit theologian Henri de Lubac, among others, took a fresh look at Origen and convinced much of the scholarly world to revise its picture of this great scholar and theologian.[31]

Faced with Gnostic exegesis, Origen insisted first on Irenaeus's solution: the guidance of the rule of faith. But as an interpreter of the whole Bible, he also worked out a method for interpreting the Scriptures.

The tendency to allegorize the Scriptures is evident even in early Christianity; we find it in the New Testament itself. The most striking example is found in the fourth chapter of Mark's Gospel: Jesus narrates the parable of the sower, and is then said to provide an explanation. The explanation is complicated, even incoherent, and anything but natural. It is probably the work of an early Christian preacher, and may stand as the first bad homily, but hardly the last. The *Didache,* to name another early example, applies to the Eucharist Jesus' words about not giving what is holy to dogs.[32]

In the second century the orthodox proposed allegories that, materially, were no different from those of the Gnostics. Irenaeus, for example, allegorizes the parable of the Good Samaritan: the man

[30] G. L. Prestige, *Fathers and Heretics: Six Studies in Dogmatic Faith with Prologue and Epilogue* (orig. publ. 1940; repr. London: SPCK, 1968) 43.

[31] See particularly Henri de Lubac, *Histoire et esprit. L'intelligence de l'Écriture d'après Origène*; Théologie, 16 (Paris: Aubier, 1950).

[32] *Didache* 9, 5, quoting Matt 7:6.

who fell among thieves is the human race, the Samaritan is Christ, the innkeeper is the Holy Spirit, and the two coins are the "image and superscription" of Father and Son imprinted on the Christian soul. Further, the coin given us (Irenaeus here invokes another parable) must produce interest.[33]

In a homily he preached on the parable of the Good Samaritan from Luke's Gospel, Origen quotes an example of allegory that he says is already traditional. The allegory left the parable with no coherent meaning:

> One of the elders who wanted to interpret the parable said this. The man who was going down is Adam. Jerusalem is paradise, and Jericho is the world. The thieves are hostile powers. The priest is the Law, the Levite is the prophets, and the Samaritan is Christ. The wounds are disobedience, the beast is the Lord's body, the *pandochium* (that is, the stable), which accepts all who wish to enter, is the Church. And further, the two denarii mean the Father and the Son. The manager of the stable is the head of the Church, to whom its care has been entrusted. And the fact that the Samaritan promises he will return represents the Savior's second coming.[34]

Origen could do better. When he begins to consider a text, he first looks carefully at its literal meaning. It is too often forgotten that spiritual exegesis, Origen's and others', is based on an utterly literal reading of the text. In Henri Crouzel's felicitous expression, the literal sense is for Origen "the brute materiality of what was said,"[35] the text read without assuming any literary figures or figurative language. Hence to speak of a "literal interpretation" would be, in Origen's mind, a contradiction in terms.

But Origen's real interest is the spiritual interpretation of Scripture. If someone knows only one passage from Origen's writings, it is probably the one where Origen says that "just as man consists

---

[33] Irenaeus, *Against the Heresies* 3, 17, 3 (SC 211, 336). The Good Samaritan: Luke 10:29-37; on the interest, Matt 25:14.

[34] Origen, *Homilies on Luke* 34, 3.

[35] Henri Crouzel, *Origène* (Paris: Lethielleux, 1985) 93. The English translator rendered Crouzel's phrase "raw matter," which misses Crouzel's point. The translation is *Origen,* trans. A. S. Worrall (San Francisco: Harper & Row, 1989) 62.

of body, soul, and spirit, so in the same way does the Scripture."[36]
The flesh of the Scripture, he writes, is "the obvious interpretation." The soul of the Scripture may edify "the man who has made some progress." The spirit is for "the man who is perfect." It is worth noting that, even in this passage, Origen does not simply say that Scripture has three parallel senses; rather, the Christian grows into the deeper senses as he progresses in the spiritual life.

The accusation most often made against Origen's exegesis—and for these purposes it is usually called "allegorical exegesis"—is that of utter arbitrariness. Origen, his critics contend, made a text mean whatever he wanted it to mean; allegorical exegesis meant the absence of any control over the interpretation of the text. Henri de Lubac, in his brilliant book on Origen's exegesis, showed how wrong this contention is. De Lubac enunciated the principle "observe Origen at work"[37]—that is, to understand Origen's method of exegesis one has to study his homilies, and not just *On First Principles*.

De Lubac showed that Origen's exegesis is anything but arbitrary. He discovered two patterns in Origen's exegesis.[38] According to the first pattern, the *historical* sense is found in an account of the events narrated in the Scriptures. The *moral* sense refers to the soul, without any necessarily Christian dimension. The *mystical* sense refers to Christ, the Church, and all the other objects of faith. The second pattern is this: the *historical* sense is found in the events of Israel's history. The *mystical* sense refers to the mystery to be fulfilled in future ages, that is, Christ and the Church. The *spiritual* sense is found in applying the text to each soul or person. This last, or "spiritual," sense differs from the "moral" of the first schema because it refers to the soul of the believer. In the believing soul, the mysteries of Christ are present and effective for the individual.

Some of what Origen wrote about the Scriptures is bizarre, although sometimes I think that Origen had a much better sense of playfulness, and even humor, than his critics do. But what is more important is that Origen provided the first Christian theological framework for the interpretation of Scripture.

[36] *On First Principles* 4, 2, 4.
[37] De Lubac, *Histoire et esprit,* 34.
[38] Ibid., 139–150.

Diodore and Theodore: The Reaction to Allegory

Origen remained, for centuries, the most respected commentator on the Bible in the Christian Church. One reason for this is the fact that he had cornered the market. He had written on most of the books of the Bible. And, in the third and fourth centuries, scholarship worked just about the way it does today: if you wanted to write a book about something, the first thing you did was to read books that others had written on the topic and take over what was good.

Toward the end of the fourth century, a kind of rebellion against Origen and his method of interpreting the Scriptures arose in the theological school at Antioch in Syria, now in the southernmost province of Turkey. The founder of the new school of interpretation was Diodore, bishop of Tarsus, who died around 390. One of his best-known pupils was Theodore, who died as bishop of Mopsuestia in 428.

Diodore and Theodore were disturbed by the extent to which the allegorical method seemed to ignore the obvious sense of the Scripture: or better, not quite ignore it, but disparage it. The Stoic philosopher Sallustius had written that the words are veils, and the truth lies beyond speech.[39] In practice, Origen had great respect for the text as a starting point and cared about the exact reading of each word. But to say that the words are veils, as Origen implied, finally makes the text evanesce, and Diodore and Theodore saw this.

In place of such a schema, Diodore and Theodore proposed another, which they expressed in a pair of Greek words, *historia* and *theória*. The *historia*, or "narrative," was the plain, literal meaning of the text, and this meaning was the base meaning. *Theória*, which means "vision" or "contemplation," added a spiritual dimension to the plain, literal meaning of the text without taking away that literal meaning. For Origen, the real meaning lay beyond the words; for Diodore and Theodore, it lay within the words. If Origen's method treated the words as veils or obstacles, Diodore and Theodore treated the words like luminescent bodies, that could be made to glow from within by *theória*. The words might glow with inner meaning, but the reader had to keep looking at the words to understand that meaning.

---

[39] See above.

Such a distinction of methods was not unique to Christians; the rabbis had carried on a similar debate. A century before Origen, Rabbi Aqiba had taught that behind every detail of the sacred text there lay a mysterious revelation. Rabbi Ishmael, in contrast, stated the principle that "The Torah speaks in the language of men."[40] The same Rabbi Ishmael went on to formulate thirteen rules for interpreting the Torah, an expansion of the seven rules of Rabbi Hillel the Elder.[41] Among Christians, the Donatist layman Tyconius also proposed seven rules of interpretation, which Augustine took over enthusiastically.[42]

Diodore, in reaction to the prevailing allegorism, wrote:

> History [or the plain literal sense] is not opposed to theôria. On the contrary, it proves to be the foundation and the basis of the higher senses. One thing is to be watched, however: theôria must never be understood as doing away with the underlying sense; it would then be no longer theôria but allegory.[43]

Theodore is more acerbic, and writes:

> There are people who take great pains to twist the senses of the divine Scriptures and make everything written therein serve their own ends. They dream up some silly fables in their own heads and give their folly the name of allegory.
>
> . . . .
>
> When they start expounding divine Scripture "spiritually"— "spiritual interpretation" is the name they like to give to their folly—they claim that Adam is not Adam, paradise is not paradise, the serpent is not the serpent. I should like to tell them this: if they make history serve their own ends, they will have no history left.[44]

---

[40] Karlfried Froelich, trans. and ed., *Biblical Interpretation in the Early Church* (Philadelphia: Fortress, 1984) 4.

[41] Ibid., 30–36.

[42] See Augustine, *On Christian Doctrine*, Book 3.

[43] Diodore of Tarsus, *Commentary on the Psalms*, Prologue, trans. in Froelich, *Biblical Interpretation*, 85.

[44] Theodore of Mopsuestia, *Commentary on Galatians 4:22-31*, trans. in Froelich, *Biblical Interpretation*, 96–97.

In some ways, Theodore revives Irenaeus's theology.[45] Theodore insists on the essential datum that God divided creation and human history into two successive ages; hence the historical context of a statement must always be taken seriously. He concludes, for example, that the Old Testament never alludes to the Trinity, and that passages that Christians take as prophetic have a clear literal sense. Only four psalms and one prophet, Malachi, predict Christ. On the other hand, he does not appeal to the rule of faith, as Irenaeus did.

Both methods had their risks. Origen risked turning the Old Testament into a blurred version of the Gospel. Theodore risked snapping the connection between Old Testament and New. In practice, Theodore and his method served more as a caution than a reform, and the Christian interpretation of the Bible in the centuries that followed moderated the excesses of Origen and his school, but never abandoned, in principle, the acceptance of a sense of Scripture that lay behind, or above, or within the literal sense.

Conclusions

What can we take from all of this? Against Gnostic distortions, Irenaeus taught that the rule of faith must be the norm for interpreting the Scriptures in the Church. Origen, the brilliant pioneer, accepted what Irenaeus taught but went beyond him, and worked out a method for interpreting the Scriptures that he applied to nearly the whole Bible. Like other pioneers, he travelled in a land that had no boundaries, and sometimes may have wandered too far afield. Diodore and Theodore offered a necessary corrective to Origen: the meaning was in the words, not beyond them. To reflect on these two methods is not to resolve all difficulties but only to begin a process. For the Scriptures nourish the Church and believing Christians, and God gave them to us so that we might have life, and have it more abundantly—the life that comes from God through Christ His Son in the Holy Spirit, to whom be glory forever.

---

[45] For what follows see Greer's work in Kugel and Greer, *Early Biblical Interpretation,* 181–182.

5 To Follow Augustine or Jerome?

The Catholic and Protestant Old Testaments

Catholics and Protestants have different canons of the Old Testament. The Jewish canon of twenty-four books is also the Protestant Old Testament canon. Catholics and the Orthodox invoke a larger canon.[1] Considering how this difference came to be will serve as one example of how complex the relation of Bible, Church, and authority can be.

For the first fifteen centuries of Christianity, no Christian Church put forth a definitive list of biblical books. Most Christians had followed St. Augustine and included the "Apocrypha" in the canon, but St. Jerome, who excluded them, had always had his defenders.[2]

---

[1] The longer canon includes Tobit, Judith, Wisdom of Solomon, Sirach (Ecclesiasticus), Baruch, 1 and 2 Maccabees, and passages in Greek added to Esther and Daniel. The Orthodox Bible also adds 1 Esdras, the Prayer of Manasseh, Psalm 151, and 3 Maccabees as deuterocanonical.

[2] See Jerome's "Preface to the Books of Samuel and Kings" (written ca. 391; English trans. by W. H. Fremantle in *The Principal Works of St. Jerome*, NPNF, 2nd series, 6 [orig. publ. 1892; repr. Grand Rapids: Eerdmans, 1954] 489–490), which he calls the "helmeted preface." It was the first preface he wrote to his "Vulgate" translation. Jerome maintains that the Old Testament has 22 books (or 24, or 27). He bases his argument on numerological considerations: there are 22 letters in the Hebrew alphabet, or 24 elders of the Apocalypse, or 27 Hebrew letters if the final letters are counted. He writes: "This preface to the Scriptures may serve as a 'helmeted' introduction to all the books which we turn from Hebrew into Latin, so that we may be assured that what is not found in our list must be placed amongst the Apocryphal

The fascinating story of how that situation changed, and what the consequences were, begins in Germany in the summer of 1519. But to understand it, we need to look at the origins of the Old Testament canon.

The Jewish Canon

A canon is a collection of writings that a community judges or believes to be authoritative. If the community is a religious one, then the collection is regarded as sacred; the Christian canon is a collection of writings regarded as normative for faith and life. But "canon" is used in other senses, too; the canon of literature, for example, that is taught in college courses is currently the subject of heated discussion.

The Greeks borrowed the word "canon" from the Semitic language group, where it meant "stalk of wheat," "cane," "reed," and then "measuring rod." In Greek the word came to mean "straight edge" or "ruler," and then "rule" or "norm."

In the early Christian Church, *kanôn* meant a "norm for distinguishing right from wrong," a "norm for behavior." The word also came to describe the confession of Christian faith and expressed "what is normative for the Church." Beginning in the fourth century, the word referred to specific things within the Church, especially to the collection of Holy Scriptures; Athanasius of Alexandria, in the fourth century, is the first to use it in this sense. In the western Church, *canon* came to mean simply "Bible" as a catalogue of ecclesiastically recognized, sacred books. The western Church also extended the use to conciliar legislation ("canon law"), the central prayer of the Eucharistic liturgy ("canon of the Mass"), and the list of recognized ("canonized") saints.

There is no Jewish concept corresponding to "canon." Negatively, the Mishnah speaks of "the external books";[3] positively, of "books that render the hands unclean."[4] The rabbis had many names for the Scriptures, among them "what is read"[5] and "the

---

writings" (ibid., 490). He then excludes Wisdom, Sirach, Judith, Tobit, the Shepherd, and 1 and 2 Maccabees. He does not mention Baruch.

   [3] *Sanhedrin* 10, 1.
   [4] *Yadaim* 3, 5.
   [5] See Neh 8:8.

books."[6] The New Testament expressions "the Scripture" and "the Scriptures" are Jewish in origin.

The final Jewish canon comprised three parts: the Law, the prophets, and the writings. Such a division becomes evident in the latter part of the second century B.C. The preface to Sirach, written around 130 B.C., calls the Scripture "the law and the prophets and the other books." In Luke 24:44, Jesus tells his disciples "that everything written about me in the law of Moses and the prophets and the psalms must be fulfilled." The Alexandrian Jew Philo writes of "laws and oracles delivered through the mouth of prophets, and psalms and the other books which foster and perfect knowledge and piety."[7] The Jewish historian Josephus counts five books of Moses, thirteen books of prophets, and four books of hymns and precepts.[8] Other passages, however, imply a two-part canon, always Law and prophets.[9] The Law and the prophets were already fixed at the time of the first centuries before and after Christ; the third part of the Jewish canon was still in flux.

The writing of the books that comprise the Hebrew Bible took place in the course of a thousand years. The process by which these writings were collected into a closed canon also lasted for centuries. According to most scholars, the collection of the Jewish Scriptures took place in three stages. The Torah, or Pentateuch, reached its final, closed form by 400 B.C., at the latest; the books of the prophets by 200 B.C.; and the writings in the course of the second century A.D.[10]

---

[6] See Dan 9:2.

[7] *On the Contemplative Life* 25 (LCL Philo 9, 127).

[8] *Against Apion* 1, 37–43 (LCL Josephus 1, 177–181).

[9] For example, 2 Macc 15:9 and 4 Macc 18:10; and in the New Testament, Matt 5:17, 7:12, 11:13, 22:40; Luke 16:16; John 1:45; Acts 13:15, 24:14, 28:23; Rom 3:21.

[10] Roger Beckwith ("Formation of the Hebrew Bible," in *Mikra: Text, Translation, Reading and Interpretation of the Hebrew Bible in Ancient Judaism and Early Christianity,* ed. Jan Martin Mulder [Philadelphia: Fortress, 1988] 39–86) dates the closing of the canon much earlier, in the time of Judas Maccabaeus (cf. 2 Macc 2:14-15), who gathered the scattered Scriptures together, so that the canon was an accomplished fact by the time of the writing of the preface to Sirach, ca. 130 B.C. (57–58). But this minority opinion is not followed here. See also Beckwith's larger work, *The Old Testament Canon of the*

The first part of the Hebrew Bible to be canonized was the Torah or Law. From the time of Abraham on, God had spoken to the leaders of his people: to the patriarchs; to Moses, Aaron, and Joshua; and to the great prophets, like Elijah and Elisha. The event closest to a written revelation was the giving of the tablets of the Law, the Ten Commandments, to Moses on Sinai. The situation began to change, however, in the late seventh century. In 621, the eighteenth year of the reign of Josiah, the "Book of the Law" was discovered in the temple.[11] This book, probably the earliest form of the present book of Deuteronomy, outlined the reform that Josiah tried to put into practice for all of Israel. For the first time, a *book* was accepted as the rule or norm of the community's life. But the acceptance of the book as normative did not preclude modification. The next significant step was taken in 444 B.C., when Ezra the Scribe read the "book of the law of Moses" (Neh 8:1) to the people, and the people accepted it, precisely as a book.[12] At least one noteworthy scholar, Bernard Anderson, holds that the Book of the Law was the Pentateuch in its final form. In any case, the Pentateuch was accepted as a closed corpus of Scripture by 400 B.C.

The second part of the canon to be fixed was the Prophets. The present Hebrew canon includes eight books under the category "prophets": Joshua, Judges, Samuel, Kings, Isaiah, Jeremiah, Ezekiel, and the Twelve. Books like Isaiah or Jeremiah originated with words that God spoke to the prophet and the prophet proclaimed to the people: "thus says the Lord," we read over and over again. Interestingly, the tradition assimilated historical books like Joshua and Samuel to prophecy, perhaps to give them divine warrant. So long as prophecy was a living tradition, these writings could be edited, and additions made; the corpus of prophetic writings was not closed. One striking example is a passage found in Isaiah: "This is the word which the Lord spoke concerning Moab in the past. But now the Lord says . . ." (Isa 16:13-14). Prophecy ceased during the third century B.C.,[13] and the corpus of the

---

New Testament Church and Its Background in Early Judaism (Grand Rapids: Eerdmans, 1985).

[11] See 2 Kgs 22–23; 2 Chr 34.

[12] See Neh 8:1–9:37.

[13] Cf. Dan 9:2: "I, Daniel, perceived in the books the number of years which, according to the word of the Lord to Jeremiah the prophet, must pass

prophets was fixed by 200 B.C. Thus the book of Daniel, for example, is not among the prophets in the Hebrew Bible.

The third group in the Jewish canon is the Writings. It is also the most diverse group. It includes the Psalms, which are the hymn book of the second temple; wisdom literature like Proverbs and Job, and short books like Esther that were read at annual festivals. The motives for closing of the third part of the canon were complex. The destruction of the temple in A.D. 70 made Judaism even more a religion of the book, so that the Writings became more significant. Pseudonymous apocalyptic writings were in circulation, and needed to be excluded. The rise of Christianity motivated a closer consideration of the canon, since Christians were using Jewish Scriptures. The Jews closed the third part of their canon sometime in the course of the second century.

The Septuagint

The canon of twenty-four Hebrew books is not the only closed collection of Jewish Scriptures. There is another one, called the "Septuagint." The Septuagint, a collection of Jewish Scriptures in the Greek language, is a fascinating point of intersection between one branch of Judaism—that is, Alexandrian Judaism—and early Christianity.[14]

The core of the Septuagint is a translation of the Hebrew Scriptures into Greek made by Jews in Alexandria, beginning in the third century B.C. The Septuagint also contains two other groups of books: translations of other books originally written in Hebrew but not found in the Hebrew canon, and books originally composed by Jews in Greek, such as the Wisdom of Solomon.

The Septuagint is in every way a remarkable undertaking.[15] It is also the first great translation project in western history, and remains one of the most interesting. But the Septuagint is much more than a translation. The Jews who made it were Alexandrians. When

---

before the end of the desolations of Jerusalem, namely, seventy years." See also Ecclesiasticus 44–50, especially the end of chapter 48 and the beginning of chapter 49.

[14] See especially Emanuel Tov, "The Septuagint," in Mulder, *Mikra*, 161–188.

[15] For this paragraph see ibid., 169–178.

they learned the Greek language, they also acquired Greek culture; and the vocabulary and concepts of the Septuagint sometimes translate not only the Hebrew language into the Greek language, but Hebrew concepts into Greek concepts. Such a translation project was utterly without precedent. The translators had neither dictionaries nor word-lists, and spoke Aramaic rather than Hebrew. Hebrew was already for them somewhat problematic, and here and there even mysterious. To establish the meaning of obscure passages, they relied on traditions of the rabbis, context, etymology, postbiblical Hebrew, Aramaic, earlier translations (especially of the Pentateuch), guesses, and—finally—giving up. The translators had to coin words for ideas like "to observe the sabbath," or "absence of circumcision," which the Greeks never needed. Technical terms like *gomer* and *ephod* were simply transliterated. Words like *manna* reflect Aramaic rather than Hebrew. Twice in the Psalms, "my wash basin" is mistranslated "basin of my hope," because a Hebrew word was misread as Aramaic. In Jeremiah, the word for "alas" is four times translated "he who is" because the translator had Exodus 3:14 in mind. In Judges 8:7 and 16, the translator gives up and writes the Hebrew word *barkonnim* in Greek letters; it probably means "briers."

Some translations, like Job, Proverbs, Isaiah, Daniel, and Esther, are free to the point of being paraphrases. Psalms, Ecclesiastes, Lamentations, Ezra-Nehemiah, and Chronicles, among others, are quite literal. Proverbs and Job are in excellent Greek, but do not reproduce the Hebrew text well. Greek Job is one-sixth shorter than the Hebrew, whereas Proverbs is expanded. Ezekiel is a translation of a Hebrew text not always well understood. Jeremiah is based on a Hebrew text different from that of the Hebrew Bible. Isaiah is so free that it can be called a "source book for ancient Jewish exegesis."[16]

In ancient times the story of how the Septuagint translation was made was told first among Jews and taken over later by Christians. As time passed the story became ever more elaborate and filled with miraculous details. According to the *Letter of Aristeas,* the elders translated only the *Law* (the Pentateuch). They finished the translation in seventy-two days, and achieved "an agreed version as the

---

[16] For this phrase, and the whole paragraph, see J. W. Wevers, "Septuagint," *Interpreters Dictionary of the Bible* 4 (1962) 276.

result of regular conference and comparison.''[17] Philo has the translators working independently of each other in separate cells. They produced seventy-two identical versions, "as though it were dictated to each by an invisible prompter," a conclusive proof of inspiration.[18] They translate only the Law. Josephus repeats the information found in the *Letter of Aristeas,* which he knows by name.[19]

The Christian Justin[20] repeats the basic narrative: Ptolemy wants the Jews' "prophetic writings" and asks King Herod—a strange anachronism—for them. Ptolemy also asks for translators. In the *Dialogue with Trypho* Justin mentions that the translation was made by seventy elders.[21] The dispute that is the occasion for Justin's remarks concerns Isaiah 7:14, which shows that, for Justin, the Septuagint was the whole Greek Old Testament. Irenaeus, too, relates that seventy elders independently produced the same translation.[22] He also knows 2 Esdras 14. Like Justin, Irenaeus was concerned with Isaiah 7:14 and asserts the superiority of the Septuagint over the translations of Thedotion and Aquila.[23]

The Septuagint is a Jewish translation and was quoted by Jewish historians, poets, and philosophers. It was also used in the synagogue. But "at the end of the first century C.E. many Jews ceased

---

[17] F. F. Bruce, *The Canon of Scripture* (Downers Grove: Intervarsity, 1988) 44. There is a complete translation of the *Letter of Aristeas* in R. H. Charles, ed., *The Apocrypha and Pseudepigrapha of the Old Testament in English,* Vol. II, *Pseudepigrapha* (Oxford: Clarendon, 1913) 94–122.

[18] *The Life of Moses* 2, 25–44 (LCL Philo 6, 461–471). Philo writes that the *Law* was translated.

[19] In *Jewish Antiquities* 12, 101–109 (LCL Josephus 7, 51–55). He copies out about two-fifths of the *Letter of Aristeas.* He is the first writer to mention the document by name and calls it *The Book of Aristeas* (ibid., 100; LCL 51). In *Jewish Antiquities* 1, 9 (LCL Josephus 4, 7) he writes that the *Law* was translated.

[20] *Apology* 1, 31, trans. Thomas B. Falls, *Saint Justin Martyr,* FC 6 (New York: Christian Heritage, 1948) 66–68.

[21] *Dialogue with Trypho* 68, 7 (trans. Falls, 258).

[22] As cited by Eusebius, *Ecclesiastical History* 5, 8, 11–15.

[23] Among later Christian fathers, Eusebius of Caesarea mentions the *Letter of Aristeas,* which he calls *Concerning the Translation of the Law by the Jews* (*Preparation for the Gospel* 9, 38), as does Epiphanius of Salamis also (*On Weights and Measures* 9).

to use the Septuagint because the early Christians had adopted it as their own translation,"[24] and it began to be considered a Christian translation. The Babylonian Talmud comments: "It happened that five elders translated the Pentateuch into Greek for King Ptolemy. That day was as hard for Israel as the day the calf was made, because the Pentateuch could not be translated properly."[25]

The Septuagint influenced the New Testament profoundly. New Testament authors quote the Septuagint and sometimes make points of belief from that translation. Terms used and even created in the Septuagint became part of the New Testament vocabulary. Because the Jews rejected it and contested its authority, the Christians became defensive about the Septuagint. Often the controverted point was Isaiah 7:14, which in the Septuagint read, "behold, a virgin shall conceive." Some Christians, ancient and modern, defended the inspiration of the Septuagint;[26] St. Augustine, for example, does so in several places.[27]

Christians and Christian beliefs did not influence the Septuagint, except in a few places, of which most did not survive. Celebrated is Justin Martyr's claim that Psalm 95 (96):10 originally read "the Lord has reigned from the tree"—that is, from the cross—and that the Jews had erased the words "from the tree."[28] Moreover, the *Vetus Latina*, or Old Latin translation (actually different translations that were in use in the West until Jerome's Vulgate replaced them) was a translation of the Septuagint. The Latin translation of the Septuagint was preserved in those parts of the Vulgate that Jerome did not translate afresh, or only revised.[29]

What has not been mentioned is the "canon" of the Septuagint, the closing of this collection of Jewish Scriptures in Greek. Earlier writers would have asserted confidently that Alexandrian Jews closed this second Jewish canon. But that claim can no longer be made; and the explanation is part of the next and last topic.

[24] Tov, "Septuagint," 163.

[25] *Massekhet Soferim* 1:7, as quoted by Tov, "Septuagint," 163.

[26] E.g. Justin Martyr; see P. Benoit, "L'Inspiration des Septante d'après les Pères," in *L'homme devant Dieu. Mélanges offerts au P. H. de Lubac* (Paris: Aubier, 1963) 169–187.

[27] Letter 28, 2; 71, 4; *On Christian Doctrine* 2, 15, 22; *City of God* 18, 43.

[28] *Dialogue with Trypho* 73, 1 (trans. Falls, 264).

[29] See Benjamin Kedar, "The Latin Translations," in Mulder, *Mikra*, 299–338.

The Two Canons after the Reformation

We return to the question, what happened in Germany in the summer of 1519?[30] In June and July of that year, Martin Luther was debating Johannes Eck at Leipzig. The topic of the debate was purgatory. Luther appealed to the Bible as the final authority. Eck quoted 2 Maccabees 12:46: "It is a holy and salutary thought to pray for the dead."[31] Luther admitted the accuracy of Eck's quotation but challenged the place of Maccabees in the canon. Eck conceded that Maccabees was not in the Hebrew canon, but appealed to the Church's canon and to Augustine. Luther appealed to Jerome and the "Hebrew verity."

Thus "Luther denied the right of the church to decide in matters of canonicity; canonicity was to be determined by the internal worth of a book."[32] Luther made the canon an acute issue for the Church, and eventually all the Reformers insisted on the shorter, Hebrew canon.

The issue did not come out of the blue. Interest in the Hebrew language and in things Jewish had been growing among Christians in Europe for more than two centuries. A near craze for the Cabala had begun in the late thirteenth century. Raymond Lull, Pico della Mirandola, and even Pope Sixtus IV were enthusiasts. Widespread persecution in the last quarter of the fifteenth century forced many Jews to convert, and they brought the Hebrew language and Jewish learning with them. At the beginning of the sixteenth century, Elias Levita published a Hebrew grammar, in Hebrew, that was widely used.[33] The Humanists became interested in the Hebrew language, and those who learned Hebrew naturally favored the Hebrew books. The Dominican Johannes Reuchlin, early in the sixteenth century, published a Hebrew grammar in Latin, and later a treatise on Hebrew accents. He was also the first modern Christian to translate a part of the Bible (the penitential psalms) directly from Hebrew. All these factors focused new attention on the

---

[30] Much of the information that follows is drawn from Albert C. Sundberg, *The Old Testament of the Early Church,* Harvard Theological Studies, 20 (Cambridge: Harvard, and London: Oxford, 1964).

[31] In the Vulgate text, "sancta est et salubris cogitatio pro defunctis exorare."

[32] Sundberg, *Old Testament,* 8.

[33] Ibid., 11–12.

shorter, Hebrew canon, and raised questions about the accuracy and value of the Latin Vulgate.

The Catholic answer to the question of the canon was given by the Council of Trent. When debate began, the limits of the canon were still an open question in the Catholic Church. Theologians at the council proposed several possibilities, including accepting the shorter canon. After debating the matter the council published (in the first decree of the fourth session, April 8, 1546) an authoritative list of the books of the Bible that included the deuterocanonical or "apocryphal" books, and added: "But if anyone does not receive these books, entire with all their parts, as they are customarily read in the Catholic Church, and are contained in the old 'vulgate' Latin edition, as sacred and canonical, . . . let him be anathema."[34] Thus the precise limits of the canon were defined authoritatively by a general council of the Catholic Church.

(An aside, to counter a common misperception. The Council of Trent did not canonize the text of the Latin Vulgate and, in 1979, the Holy See published the "New Vulgate," a Latin translation of the Bible in line with the original Hebrew, Aramaic, and Greek texts for use in Latin liturgies.)

The history of the Protestant position is more complex. The Protestants had rejected any central authority for doctrine and feared human judgment passed on the word of God. Since they could not appeal to authority, they made the only appeal they could: to history.

In the course of four centuries, three main arguments emerged in succession. First: the New Testament quotes only the books of the shorter canon, and Jesus and the apostles thus defined the Christian Old Testament. Second: the Jews closed the canon in the fifth century B.C. at the Great Synagogue in the time of Ezra the Scribe, and this ancient canon is the only authentic one. Third: the Jews had two canons: a shorter one in Palestine and a longer one in Alexandria, and the Palestinian canon is the more authentic one.

Each argument was an attempt to defend Protestant belief and practice on historical grounds, and each was also a polemical stance against the Catholic teaching at Trent. But the men who proposed

---

[34] Text in *Conciliorum oecumenicorum decreta*, ed. Giuseppe Alberigo et al. (Bologna: Istituto per le Scienze Religiose, 1973) 664.

the arguments were also scholars and in the end their own historical research, slowly but surely, eroded the ground from under them.

The argument that the New Testament authors had not used apocryphal literature began to break down in the early eighteenth century. In 1713, G. Surenhusius published, in Amsterdam, the first collection of evidence for the use of apocrypha in the New Testament. In 1828, the German E. R. Stier, overcome perhaps by enthusiasm, published a collection of 102 New Testament passages that resembled the Apocrypha. Later scholars pared the list down, and G. Wildeboer eventually divided the evidence into three categories: (1) reminiscences of apocryphal writings, (2) information derived from apocryphal sources and treated like the Old Testament, and (3) actual quotations.[35] Critical scholarship had provided the facts, and the facts could not be ignored: the New Testament made extensive use of apocryphal literature. So the thesis that the New Testament writings established the Old Testament canon had to be abandoned.

The second argument maintained that the Jews had closed their canon in the time of Ezra. Elias Levita, in the early sixteenth century, was the first to propose it. He based his theory on passages from the Talmud, and provided much detail: Ezra and his associates had joined twenty-four books into one volume and divided them into Law, Prophets, and Writings. They had the original, autograph copies of the books from Moses and the Prophets. The men of the Great Synagogue even introduced the "Qere," or marginal substitutions—but not, interestingly, the vowel points, which Levita attributed to the Masoretes (about A.D. 500).[36]

Again, historical research undid the thesis. The Great Synagogue turned out to be, in fact, an anachronism, not attested earlier than the second century A.D. Critical study also showed that several books of the Hebrew canon—Daniel is the best example—had to be dated centuries after the time of Ezra. In 1876, Abraham Kuenen, in an article published in Dutch, definitively refuted the theory of the Great Synagogue, and with it the hypothesis of an early closing of the Hebrew canon.[37]

---

[35] Sundberg, *Old Testament,* 26.

[36] Ibid., 12–14.

[37] Abraham Kuenen, "Over de mannen des Groote Synagoge," in *Verslagen en Mededeelingen der Koninklijke Akademie van Wetenschappen* (Amsterdam, 1876)

The third thesis had a longer life. The man who first proposed it was Johann Salomo Semler (1725–1791), a professor of Protestant theology at Halle. Semler had undertaken the first strictly historical investigation of the canon and was not engaged in anti-Catholic polemics. To explain the fact that a large part of the Christian Church had accepted the longer canon, he postulated the following: in the time of Jesus, the Jews had two canons of Scripture: a shorter canon, in Palestine (the current Hebrew Bible or Protestant Old Testament) and a longer one, in Alexandria (the Septuagint, or Catholic Old Testament). Gentile Christians, who soon predominated, took over the closed canon of the Hellenistic Jews.[38] Semler even believed that the seventy men who translated the Septuagint into Greek were inspired.

But Protestants, for a century after Semler, continued to maintain that the Great Synagogue had closed the canon, and hence rejected Semler's theory. The standard formulation was this: Ezra and the Great Synagogue closed the canon. The books of the Apocrypha were written in Greek at a late date, and only the ignorant and uninformed among the Jews read them. Jesus and his apostles made the Hebrew canon the Church's Old Testament. Only after the time of Justin (around A.D. 160) did some Christians use the Apocrypha, but they never considered them canonical. The Roman Catholic Church made the Apocrypha canonical at Trent, and committed a terrible error: it tampered with God's Word.[39]

Once Kuenen had refuted the theory of the Great Synagogue, however, Semler's theory of the double canon quickly found general acceptance. It explained the existence of a double Old Testament in Christianity, and it still made the Palestinian Hebrew canon sound more authentic. The theory is still widely accepted.

A few decades ago, however, the American scholar Albert Sundberg, in a book that deserves more attention, demonstrated a significant problem with the theory of a closed Alexandrian canon

---

207–248; German translation by K. Budde in *Gesammelte Abhandlungen zur biblischen Wissenschaft von Dr. Abraham Kuenen* (Freiburg i. Br., 1894) 125–160. See Sundberg, *Old Testament*, 33.

[38] Ibid., 3–4.
[39] Ibid., 23.

in Judaism: namely, that there is no evidence for it.[40] (The theory of the Alexandrian canon is not the only instance in which German scholarship has erected a magnificent structure without anyone's noticing that the building lacked a ground floor.)

Sundberg's hypothesis is this:[41] before Christianity began, Judaism had fixed the corpus of the Law and the Prophets, but had no closed canon. "Writings" were still being composed, translated, and circulated. Around A.D. 100, Palestinian Jews closed the third group of Scriptures, the "Writings," and thus established the current Hebrew canon. The Christians, meanwhile, had inherited an open canon from Judaism. They—and this is Sundberg's distinctive, even revolutionary hypothesis—closed their own Old Testament canon. Put another way, the Septuagint is an exclusively Christian canon, and it may even be considered the Christian Old Testament. In other words, Sundberg proposes that Hebrew canon and the Septuagint are not two Jewish canons, one Palestinian and rabbinic, the other Alexandrian and Hellenistic, but rather that the Hebrew canon and the Septuagint are half-brothers, both begotten by the same Father but born of different mothers. Sundberg's thesis, of course, has further implications for the Christian Church, but they need not concern us here.

Conclusions

From this example of the two canons, I would like to draw some conclusions about the Bible, the Church, and authority.

It is easy to caricature both positions: for Catholics, the Bible is whatever the Church says it is, and for Protestants, the Bible is whatever the individual believer wants it to be: one infallible pope versus uncounted infallible believers, authoritarian objectivity versus libertarian subjectivity. But these are precisely caricatures.

Catholics do, it seems to me, take more readily to a community, and more readily trust in a community. Protestants, in matters of faith, are rather individualists, eager to encounter God in Scripture without any mediator.

Both positions raise further questions. No Catholic would want to say that the authority of the Bible derives simply from the de-

[40] Ibid., 81.
[41] Ibid., 82.

cree of a council. Trent recognized the Bible; it did not create it. The Bible is in the Church, but not from the Church, and the Church is subject to God's Word. St. Augustine's statement, "I would not believe the Gospel unless the authority of the Catholic Church moved me to this,"[42] is often misused. Yet Catholics need to explain the relationship between the authority of the Bible and the authority of the Church. Faith can and must seek understanding.

The Protestant understanding of the Bible is different. Luther had appealed to the inner worth of a book as the criterion for canonicity, and the Reformers came to regard the inner witness of the Holy Spirit as the final proof of scriptural inspiration.[43] Yet the Protestant Churches, in fact, accept and use a uniform canon. They need to explain why. Many Protestants accept the canon as a historical fact rather than as a doctrine. And the Lutheran distinction between Law and Gospel shifts the focus from the precise limits of the canon to the presence of Gospel in the Bible as distinct from the Law that is also there. Such a position stands in contrast to the Catholic insistence on *tota scriptura*, "the whole of Scripture."

In other words, the fixed barriers erected during the Reformation and Counter-Reformation are being breached. In this as in all our endeavors, may the name of God, who spoke his Word to us in the Holy Spirit, be praised forever.

---

[42] "Ego vero Evangelio non crederem, nisi me catholicae Ecclesiae commoveret auctoritas"; *Against the Letter of Manichaeus Entitled "Fundamental"* 5, 6 (PL 42, 176).

[43] R. H. Pfeiffer, "Canon of the OT," *Interpreter's Dictionary of the Bible* 1 (1962) 518.

6 Word of God or Human Works?

Inspiration, Inerrancy, and the Canon of Scripture

The authority of the Bible is easier to assert than to explain. From bumper stickers to sides of barns and banners held up at football games, many people are convinced that they need only quote the Bible and its truth and authority will be obvious.

But it's not that simple. Like most things worth thinking about, the idea of "authority" is considerably more complex than it appears to be. I'd like to consider the concept of "authority" in itself first, and then turn to the authority of the Bible.

The Nature of Authority

"Authority" is not a welcome word these days. "Authority" makes us think of someone pointing a finger and saying: "Do it—not because it's reasonable or because you want to, but because I told you to."

In this form "authority" is perceived as a synonym for "oppression," and rebellion against authority is admired. We hear about a crisis of authority. Children question their parents' authority. The authority of the state is challenged. The authority of the past is disparaged. And for the past twenty-five years, the hottest topic in Catholic theology in America has been the nature and limits of authority in the Church.

Perhaps the saddest aspect of the crisis of authority is distrust of internal authority, the strength of one's own convictions. A generation of college students has been so anesthetized by relativism that they cannot say that Shakespeare was the greatest master of the English language for fear of offending someone who thinks that Danielle Steel is. But if they can never say, "You are wrong," they can never say "I am right," either.

Nevertheless, the explosion of knowledge has made us increasingly dependent on authority. A noteworthy example is the authority of "medical research," which has a mesmerizing effect on so many people. The same free-range yuppies who wear all-cotton T-shirts that say "Question Authority" read an article about oat bran and rush out to buy oat-bran doughnuts. An op-ed piece entitled: "Alarm Clocks Can Kill You. Have a Smoke" appeared recently in the New York *Times*. The author surveyed three issues of ten magazines and found articles about the fearful dangers to health that lurk in such things as imported fresh fruit, alarm clocks, dinnerware, hot tubs, roller coasters, and smiles; the same magazines, she writes, carried just under two hundred ads for cigarettes.[1]

But "authority" is an important concept, and it deserves a better analysis. As a way of beginning to understand it, three examples will show some of the range of its meaning.

One is this: you're sitting in your car waiting for someone. A policeman walks up and says, "Move your car, now." You don't like him or his manners, and it's inconvenient for you to move the car. But you do it. By moving your car, you acknowledge a purely external, formal authority. You obey the policeman not because you like him, or because moving your car makes any sense to you, but simply because he is a policeman.

Another example: a woman says to her husband, "Kiss me." Grammatically, she uses the imperative; she gives a command. But if her husband loves her, he hardly experiences what she says as a command. Her authority blends in so completely with his wishes and desires that it becomes internal to him; kissing her not only makes sense to him, but delights him.

A third case: a man wearing the obligatory black jacket points a revolver at your chest and says, "Give me your wallet." Is this just a more extreme case of the policeman who says, "Move your car, now"? Clearly not. What distinguishes the policeman from the mugger? Both the policeman and the mugger exercise power.

[1] Elizabeth M. Whelan, "Alarm Clocks Can Kill You. Have a Smoke," New York *Times,* September 8, 1992, op-ed page.

Authority *is* a kind of power: the policeman does get you to move the car. But the exchange with the policeman has an element that the exchange with the mugger does not: that element is freedom, at least a residual sort of freedom. Freedom here does not mean "I can do whatever I want to." You are not eager to move your car, but you do. In the case of the mugger, one cannot speak even of a residual freedom, but only the fear of being shot.

Thus there are two key questions in trying to define authority. One is how to distinguish authority from power. The other is to understand how authority is related to freedom.

Authority is clearly a kind of power. It can be called legitimate power, or just power. Authority operates within the ambit of freedom, at least in a minimal sense: the response to authority always includes some residue of human freedom. Once the last vestige of freedom is suppressed, authority is supplanted by brute power.

What finally rightly commands obedience is truth. Nicholas Lash has written, "Ultimately, the only authority is the authority of truth; the truth that is God, the source and ground of all truth."[2] He had a precedent in Augustine, who wrote: "And surely the highest authority is that of the truth itself when it is clearly known."[3] And truth is finally liberating: in Jesus' words, "You will know the truth, and the truth will make you free" (John 8:32). St. Augustine was able to describe the blessed life of heaven as "joy in the truth."[4] Real authority is not arbitrary, because the final authority is the truth. Moreover, authority is not an end in itself. It is rather the means to achieving true freedom.

Further, because truth is by nature intelligible, all authority, even divine authority, can be authenticated. Thus the question of the authority of the Bible can and should be asked.

When reflecting on authority, some distinctions are useful. For example, authority can be personal or impersonal. But behind every impersonal authority is a personal authority; impersonal authority is always the fixed residue of personal authority. For example, the hexagonal red sign at an intersection that reads "STOP" is impersonal. But a personal authority stands behind it—the traffic commissioner, or the city council. The distinction between personal

---

[2] Nicholas Lash, *Voices of Authority* (Shepherdstown: Patmos, 1976) 24.
[3] *On True Religion* 24, 45.
[4] *Confessions* 10, 23, 33.

and impersonal authority will be important when we ask about the
authority of the Bible.

Moreover, personal authority can be external or internal. The
policeman has authority because of his office, not because of his
person, whereas the scientist who delivers a learned paper is
authoritative because of who he is.

External personal authority can be juridical or moral. When the
president calls citizens to serve in the army in time of war, he is
exercising an external, personal authority that is juridical. When
a mother tells her little daughter, "Clean up your room and put
away your toys," her external, personal authority is moral rather
than juridical. Whether the president or the mother has more suc-
cess, I leave up to you.

Thus, when we consider the concept of authority a little more
carefully, we see that it has a wide range of applications. Authority
is always the legitimate power to command assent or obedience.
At one end of the spectrum, authority ends when the last vestige
of freedom is suppressed. At that point authority becomes brute
power. At the other end of the spectrum is the Beatific Vision:
when I shall behold the face of God in all its beauty, no one will
need to command me to adhere to the Good. I shall find the Good
so utterly desirable and lovable that any last need for authority will
fall away.

Authority in Church and State

A glance at the history of western thought shows that the need
to justify authority, and hence the impulse to reflect on it, arose
only after the Reformation, which spurred reflection, first on the
nature of authority in the Church, and then on authority in the
state.

The Greeks and the Romans simply assumed that authority is
necessary and never speculated much about it.

There is no one Hebrew word for "authority" in the Old Testament. The Old Testament recognizes God's authority as absolute:
it is everlasting, universal, unquestionable (Dan 4:34-35). God com-
municates his authority to human beings such as judges, priests,
kings, and prophets. Other cultures made their kings divine; Israel
saw the judge and the king as holding delegated authority and hence

bound by justice and righteousness. By the later years of the monarchy, written Scriptures were also accepted as authoritative.

According to the New Testament, too, God's authority is absolute and unique, an aspect of his unalterable, universal, eternal dominion over his world. Paul compares God's authority to the potter's authority over the clay (Rom 9:21). Jesus and all his followers acknowledged the authority of the Jewish Scriptures. In St. Matthew's Gospel, Jesus says: "all authority in heaven and on earth has been given to me" (Matt 28:18). He gave his disciples authority, and Paul writes of "the authority the Gospel gives me" (1 Cor 9:18 NAB).

With the passing of time many other forms of authority developed in the Church. Some provided norms for the truths of faith, others regulated life and action. Examples are the canon of Scripture, creeds, the decrees of councils and synods, bishops and the pope, the Fathers of the Church, doctors of the Church, and canon law.

Christianity also taught that the legitimate authority of the state was ultimately from God, and it was generally inclined to submit to it. Christians did recognize, however, that the state could abuse its authority, and in such cases they had to resist, as the martyrs attest.

The Reformers rejected all claims to religious authority except that of the Bible, including the authority of philosophy, tradition, and Church hierarchy. *Sola Scriptura* was much more than a slogan. By their doctrines of the equal priesthood of all believers, and of the Inner Light as the final authority, they also denied that the Church is the one authentic interpreter of Scripture. Early Reformers did appeal to other norms, such as the consensus of the first five centuries, or the first four ecumenical councils, but such claims were soon abandoned. The principle of *sola Scriptura* meant that all the eggs were in one basket, and Protestantism had to be very careful about what happened to that basket: if the Bible was the only authority, then a very careful defense of biblical authority had to be worked out.[5]

Philosophical reflection on the authority of the state generally followed the lines of the Protestant principle. Both Thomas Hobbes

---

[5] See also C. H. Dodd, *The Authority of the Bible,* 2nd ed. (New York: Harper, 1958) 20, for a good formulation of this problem.

(1588–1679) and Jean-Jacques Rousseau (1712–1778) proposed forms of the social contract. For Hobbes, individuals yield their right of self-government to a commonwealth, "that great Leviathan, that mortal god." For Rousseau, the source of all political authority and all true sovereignty derives from the people as a whole; yet Rousseau, too, thought that he needed to divinize the legislator.

Protestants had invested a great deal in *sola Scriptura*. But rationalism and historicism chipped away at the authority of all norms. After the peak of Protestant orthodoxy at the turn of the eighteenth century, Protestant theologians became increasingly defensive about the authority of Scripture. With the liberal theology of men like Friedrich Schleiermacher and the new biblical criticism that arose from historicism, the authority of the Bible was radically questioned. With the rise of historical biblical criticism, "reason" became practically the only norm for authority.

Others attempted to appeal to religious experience as authoritative. But again, criteria for judging experience are necessary, unless one is ready to accept St. Theresa of Avila and Mary Baker Eddy on the same footing.

Catholics perceived authority as distributed among Bible, tradition, and the Church. This Catholic principle postponed the discussion of biblical authority, but only for a time. The problems of biblical authority that Protestants had raised were fiercely debated in the Catholic Church during the Modernist crisis at the end of the nineteenth century and the beginning of the twentieth.

Authority and Inspiration

What is the Bible's authority? A whole range of answers can be collected, from saying that every word of the Bible is literally true to saying that it is true in the way that all great literature, like Sophocles' *Oedipus Rex,* Dante's *Divine Comedy,* or Shakespeare's *Hamlet,* is true. Most Christians would agree on the statement, "The Bible is authoritative"—that is, it can rightly and worthily command loyalty and obedience. But to say that the Bible is authoritative is to begin a discussion, not to end it.

Christian theology has several terms for talking about the authority of the Bible. One is "canon." Another is "inspiration." Others are "inerrancy" and "infallibility." "Inspiration" is the fundamental category. Inerrancy and infallibility are consequences drawn from the affirmation of inspiration, which bring out particular aspects and implications of inspiration.

To say that the books of the Bible are "canonical" is to say that they are "normative" for Christian faith and life; "canon," etymologically, means "norm." To say that the Bible is authoritative because it is canonical is to assign impersonal authority to it, the authority that stands behind the red "STOP" sign. But behind all impersonal authority is personal authority: in the case of the "STOP" sign, the city council; in the case of the Bible, God.

The most common way of talking about God's personal authority as standing behind the Bible is with the term "inspiration." Because God inspired it, the Bible speaks with God's authority.

In its root meaning, "inspiration" means "breathing into." It implies that God, or some divine force, affects a speaker, a writer, or a text. The inspiration of the Bible is such a familiar concept to contemporary Christians that we can easily assume it has always been important. It has not. The modern dispute is just that—modern. The Fathers of the Church made many incidental comments about inspiration, but never reflected on it as such, and certainly never wrote books about it. The same is true, for example, of Thomas Aquinas: he never wrote a treatise on inspiration but included his remarks on it in what he wrote about prophecy. Theological speculation on inspiration, among both Protestants and Catholics, began only after the first waves of the Reformation and Counter-Reformation.

In order to be concise and, to some extent at least, comprehensible, I would like to summarize modern theories of inspiration, both Protestant and Catholic—and most positions are found in writers of both confessions—under four headings:[6] verbal inspiration and total inerrancy, verbal inspiration and religious inerrancy, the inspiration of ideas or persons, and social inspiration.

"Verbal inspiration and total inerrancy" is the theory that the whole Bible is inspired by God in such a way that divine authority guarantees the truth of each word.

Maintaining strict verbal inspiration, which is also called plenary inspiration, is typical of many evangelical Protestants. The the-

---

[6] The headings and some of the data that follow are adapted from Robert Gnuse, *The Authority of the Bible: Theories of Inspiration, Revelation, and the Canon of Scripture* (New York/Mahwah: Paulist, 1985).

ory holds that the Bible is infallible or inerrant in every aspect, including incidental points of history and science. Some of its proponents speak of inspiration as dictation by God to a human scribe. The doctrine arose in the seventeenth century and, in the United States, was elaborated at Princeton Seminary in the nineteenth. Its best-known American proponent was Benjamin Warfield.[7]

The reasoning of those who hold strict verbal inspiration proceeds this way:[8] If God is truthful, and Scripture is God's revelation, then Scripture must be true in all its parts. If God is faithful to his Church, then he must have given his Church a trustworthy guide to belief and practice. Hence Scripture can be trusted to guide every belief and action of a Christian.

Proponents of strict verbal inspiration usually connect their view of the Scriptures as divine with insistence on Christ's full divinity, often to the neglect of his humanity. If Jesus implied, for example, that Moses wrote the Pentateuch, or that one author wrote the Book of Isaiah, or that Jonah lived three days in the belly of a whale, then these propositions are guaranteed as true. Warfield described strict verbal inspiration with an alluring metaphor: it is like brilliant sunlight passing through a stained-glass window and appearing to the eye in many colors.[9] But the metaphor is only alluring: the stained glass adds nothing to the sunlight, but only limits it.

Proponents of verbal inspiration take the Bible utterly seriously and show the greatest respect for it. But they see science as the enemy of religion. They often propose teaching creation-science in schools, and acclaim triumphantly that archaeological discoveries confirm the truth of the Bible. Faced with of textual criticism, they sometimes hold that only the original copy, the autograph, was inerrant.

For many proponents of strict verbal inspiration, the defense of Scripture can become more important than Scripture itself. The theology that they insist is the clear and obvious teaching of the Bible is often nineteenth-century conservative Protestant doctrine.

[7] On evangelical Protestants, see Frederick W. Norris's illuminating book *The Apostolic Faith: Protestants and Roman Catholics* (Collegeville: The Liturgical Press, 1992). The book presents the Tuohy Lectures for 1988.

[8] Summarized from Gnuse, *Authority,* 25–26.

[9] Benjamin Warfield, *The Inspiration and Authority of the Bible* (repr. Philadelphia: Presbyterian and Reformed, 1948) 156.

Many Christians find that a doctrine of strict verbal inspiration is not only untenable, but a distortion: it denies the humanity of the Bible just as it denies the humanity of Christ.

The theory of "verbal inspiration and religious inerrancy" holds that the whole Bible should be called inspired, but that only the *religious* teachings of the Bible are inerrant and infallible, whereas divine authority does not stand behind historical or scientific assertions.

The doctrine of limited verbal inspiration was common among the Fathers of the Church, who called it "accommodation." They explained that the language of the Bible was pedagogical: God spoke to his people as a parent speaks to a child. Luther and Calvin both appealed to accommodation, as did many Catholics in the nineteenth century. Catholics often used the categories "efficient cause" and "instrumental cause" to explain limited verbal inspiration: God was the principal author of Scripture, and the human authors were the instruments he used. Precisely because they were human, and not merely pens or pencils, the human dimension of the Bible can be accounted for. In this century Catholics have been fairly willing to say that the interpretation of the Bible needs to take into account progress in the understanding of history and science; the different literary forms, with their own rules, that the biblical authors used; the authors' original intent; and the relation of a single passage or book to the whole of the Bible.

A doctrine of limited verbal inspiration allows the Bible to be treated as a religious work; in one old phrase, the Bible teaches "how to go to heaven, and not how the heavens go."

The problem with this view is applying it. It is easy to say that religious teachings are inspired, while historical and scientific assertions are not. But who is to decide which is which? To take one point that is currently sharply debated: in the New Testament Jesus calls God "Father" more than 150 times. Is the Fatherhood of God an infallible religious teaching, or is it a culturally conditioned historical phenomenon that can be accommodated to modern sensibilities?

"The inspiration of ideas or persons" holds that inspiration is to be predicated not of the words of the Bible but of its ideas or content or, alternatively, of its authors.

"Inspiration of ideas" can be summed up in the phrase, "The ideas are God's, the words are man's." Both Protestants and Catholics proposed it, but it flourished especially among Catholics in the nineteenth century. Among its best-known proponents were John Henry Newman and Cardinal Johannes Franzelin. Franzelin taught that the authors of Scripture received their ideas, thoughts, and judgment from God, but created the words and phrases themselves. Newman[10] held that Scripture was authoritative in matters of faith and morals, but that the rest of the text might contain human error. "The entirety of Scripture is inspired insofar as it relates to religion," is one author's summary of Newman.[11] Newman compared the divine and the human in Scripture to the divine and the human in the sacraments, such as water and grace in baptism. But for Newman, biblical authority was not the ultimate concern, because the Church taught the truth and Scripture verified its teaching.

"Inspiration of ideas" avoids the pitfalls of verbal inspiration and centers attention on the central religious message of the Bible. But it does not contain a method for discerning what the inspired ideas are. To give only one example, Christians differ sharply over the question whether salvation is appropriated by sacramental baptism in water or by accepting Christ as one's personal Savior. Which is the central religious teaching?

Moreover, the suggestion that ideas and words can be detached from each other is suspect. We might have good ideas for sonnets, but probably have not written the likes of what Shakespeare wrote. To use a more recent example, in one of Philip Roth's novels the main character—who happens to be a successful novelist—is pursued throughout the book by a man with a manuscript wrapped in brown paper, who keeps saying to him, "I have a great novel here, you just put in the right words." That's the stuff of nightmares.

The theory that God inspires the authors rather than what they wrote is more typically Protestant. Its proponents included Johann Gottfried Herder in Germany, Harry Emerson Fosdick in the United States, and Charles Dodd in England. The theory sees the authors as "religious geniuses," and the Bible as the record of their communion with the divine. The theory has the appeal that all mysticism has, but ultimately it holds that not the canon of Scripture, but religious genius, is normative.

[10] See James Tunstead Burtchaell, *Catholic Theories of Biblical Inspiration since 1810: A Review and Critique* (Cambridge: University Press, 1969) 65–79.
[11] Ibid., 73.

The theory of "social inspiration" holds that inspiration is a charism bestowed upon an entire community rather than upon words, ideas, or writers.

James Barr holds such a theory of social inspiration. It is also common among contemporary Catholics, among whom Karl Rahner stands out.

Rahner calls Scripture "the objectification of the church of the apostolic age which is normative for us,"[12] and writes that "the church of the apostolic age objectifies itself in scripture."[13] The Church does not make the biblical books canonical, or endow them with their inspired character—a notion that Vatican I rejected[14]— yet only the Church's teaching makes their canonicity and inspiration known.

Rahner appears to be rejecting the implications of *Frühkatholizismus,* "early Catholicism"—the notion that an ideal, and purely Christian, Church existed in the first decades but soon relapsed part way into Judaism and became institutionalized as "Catholic." He rather sees both Church and canon as evolving during the earliest decades, like an unstable cell in the process of dividing. "The real theological essence of the church is constituted in a historical process in which the church comes to the fullness of this essence and to the possession of this essence in faith."[15] Such a self-constitution implies written objectifications. "Therefore this process is *also,* but not exclusively, the process of the formation of the canon."[16]

Not everything in the original Church is, or can be, normative for the faith and life of the Church throughout its earthly existence. Yet the Church in every age remains bound to its origins. It is pre-

[12] Karl Rahner, *Foundations of Christian Faith: An Introduction to the Idea of Christianity,* trans. William V. Dych (New York: Seabury, 1978) 371.

[13] Ibid., 372.

[14] "But the Church holds [the books of the Old and New Testaments] as sacred and canonical not because they were composed by human industry alone and for this reason are approved by the Church's authority, nor because they contain revelation without error, but because, since the Holy Spirit inspired [them], they have God as their author, and as such have been given to the Church itself." Vatican Council I, *Dogmatic Constitution on the Catholic Faith,* ch. 2.

[15] Rahner, *Foundations,* 373.

[16] Ibid.

cisely in the canon of Scripture that the Church objectifies itself, and thus the Scripture is normative for all ages. Far from seeing the Church lapsing into an inferior state around A.D. 150 or 200, when the canon of the New Testament is clearly established, Rahner sees it having passed through infancy, childhood, and adolescence, and reaching a young but definitive maturity, precisely at that moment at which the principle, at least, of a canon is established.

Of inspiration Rahner writes:

> If the church was founded by God himself through his Spirit and in Jesus Christ, if the *original* church as the norm for the future church is the object of God's activity in a qualitatively unique way which is different from his preservation of the church in the course of history, and if scripture is a constitutive element of this original church as the norm for future ages, then this already means quite adequately and in both a positive and an exclusive sense that God is the author of scripture and that he inspired it.[17]

In its general form social inspiration asserts that everyone involved in producing the Bible was inspired. Karl Rahner, in his specific version of social inspiration, holds that inspiration is a unique function of the apostolic Church. God establishes the original community of faith, and the community produces the Scriptures. Hence, the Scriptures are the uniquely authoritative deposit of tradition. God is the principal author of the Scriptures, and the Church is the secondary author. The Bible can exist as Scripture only in the Church; the Bible is the Church's book.

Rahner's answer is seductively appealing to a Catholic, because it does a good job of putting three important Catholic themes— Scripture, tradition, and Church—into a harmonious relationship. But its implications should not be missed. For Rahner, the Church produces the Bible; it is difficult to see how the Church is not primary, the Scriptures secondary. The Bible is, and remains, the Church's book, and the Bible can exist as Scripture only in the Church. Rahner also maintains the Catholic insistence on Scripture and tradition as the bearers of revelation. Many recent Protestant authors have also faced up to the need to discuss the role of tradition, at least in the formation of the canon: the only way

[17] Ibid., 374.

we know what books belong to the Bible is by tradition; the Bible does not justify itself.

The problem that Rahner, and, more generally, any theory of social inspiration, leaves, is this: what is finally inspired, the Bible or the community that formed it? The theory runs the risk of sidestepping the question whether the Bible itself can be called inspired.

Conclusions: The Authority of the Bible

Christians consider the Bible authoritative. That is certain. How is the Bible authoritative?

We might begin by applying the analysis of authority to the Bible. The Bible exercises authority, not power, because it does not force itself on anyone. The authority, or legitimate power, of the Bible is the power of the truth to persuade freely. In the belief of many Christians—St. Augustine and Karl Barth are two that stand out—a call from God must precede an individual's free acceptance of the truth of the Bible. What validates the authority of the Bible? If the Bible is viewed as an impersonal authority, then it is authoritative insofar as it is a canon. As canon, it is validated by the Church, or by God. (I pass over a thorny question here.) If the authority behind the Bible is seen as personal, then God validates its authority. God's validating authority is usually called "inspiration." God's authority must be both external and internal at the same time. He is both Creator and Lord, and absolute Truth. He commands obedience, and obeying him is the essence of intelligibility. Yet the Bible is also expressed in human words, by human authors. This Bible is not simply God's Word, devoid of any human element, unless one wants to accept the consequences of strict verbal inspiration.

Inspiration is finally a mystery, in the theological sense of that word: a truth of our faith that we can always understand better, but never fully penetrate. Perhaps the best analogy is the person of Christ: Christ is true God and true man, yet one person. So the Scriptures are the word of God and the word of man, yet one utterance.

Theories of strict verbal inspiration try to ignore the human words. Theories of social inspiration are attractive, but seem to skirt the precise problem of inspired Scripture. The right answer seems to lie in the area staked out as limited verbal inspiration and inspiration of ideas. In both cases, the problem was the need for a criterion by which the inspired message can be discerned and distinguished from the incidental details. The quest for such a criterion was not a vain one, as we shall see. To the living and eternal Word of God the Father be honor and glory in the Holy Spirit forever.

7 Holy Bible or Holy Church?

The New Testament Canon in Recent Theology

We come to the last of these lectures with a question about the present: Why should the Christian Church retain its New Testament canon of twenty-seven books?

To begin to understand the question, we might ask whether the present canon could be expanded, or shortened.

Suppose a letter were discovered that was clearly and obviously by St. Paul. We know, for example, that he wrote at least two letters to the Corinthians that have been lost. If such a letter were found somewhere—we might call it "One and a Half Corinthians"—would it belong to the New Testament?

Or, can the canon be shortened? Paul's little Letter to Philemon, for example, clearly condones slavery: Paul sends the runaway slave Onesimus back into slavery under his owner Philemon. Should Philemon be dropped from the canon? No witness to any important Christian doctrine would be lost, and a small embarrassment would be eliminated from the canon.

These questions are not my main point, but let me say a few words about them.

For the Catholic Church, the Council of Trent decreed that the twenty-seven books, entire and with all their parts, are sacred and canonical, but does not explicitly exclude other books. So the Catholic canon could hardly be shortened, but it might be lengthened, although it is difficult to imagine that happening.

Most Protestants who ask the question answer that the canon must in principle remain open, because no human authority can close it.[1]

---

[1] For example, Karl Barth writes, "An absolute guarantee that the history of the Canon is closed, and therefore that what we know as the Canon is also

The Authority of the New Testament Canon in Recent Theology

By far the more interesting question is this: What do Christian theologians say when asked, why should the Church maintain this canon of twenty-seven books? I'd like to survey some of the answers that have been given since about 1950. Most of the theologians are Protestant, and many are German. Some profound reflection on the canon took place in German Protestant theology in the years after 1950, and this thought is worth considering.

The precise question is this: Is this collection of twenty-seven books, as a collection, authoritative? If so, how is its authority explained?

I will answer by a series of disjunctions. Either the New Testament canon is authoritative, or it is not. If it is authoritative, then its authority is confirmed by criteria that are either internal or external to it. If its authority is confirmed by criteria that are internal to it, then these criteria are either the whole of the Scripture or part of it. If its authority is confirmed by criteria that are external to it, then these criteria are either historical or dogmatic.

I will try to explain each possibility and then illustrate it from the work of one or several theologians.

The most radical position to be found on the authority of the canon was proposed by Herbert Braun, professor of New Testament at the University of Mainz, in an article he published in 1960;[2] more than a few other authors tacitly assume the same position. The title of the article is "Does Contemporary New Testament Exegetical Research Abolish the Canon?" Braun's answer is: yes, it does. He argues that contemporary exegetes have demonstrated such ir-

---

closed, cannot be given either by the Church or by individuals in the Church according to the best and most satisfactory answers to this question." Karl Barth, *The Doctrine of the Word of God*; Church Dogmatics I, 2, trans. G. T. Thomson and Harold Knight (Edinburgh: T&T Clark, 1956) 476.

   [2] Herbert Braun, "Hebt die heutige neutestamentlich-exegetische Forschung den Kanon auf?" First published in *Fuldaer Hefte* 12 (1960) 9–24. Reprinted in H. Braun, *Gesammelte Studien zum Neuen Testament und seiner Umwelt* (Tübingen: J.C.B. Mohr [Paul Siebeck], 1962) 310–324, and in Ernst Käsemann, ed., *Das Neue Testament als Kanon. Dokumentation und kritische Analyse zur gegenwärtigen Diskussion* (Göttingen: Vandenhoeck & Ruprecht, 1970) 219–232.

reconcilable contradictions within the New Testament that the New Testament cannot be considered a unity, and the canon therefore disintegrates. Some of his examples are these. Jesus, Paul, and the author of the Fourth Gospel reject the observance of the Torah as a way to salvation; Matthew, Luke, Hebrews, Acts, and the Pastorals reintroduce the observance of law as a way of salvation. Or: Jesus and Paul expected the coming of judgment and the Kingdom in their own generation; Luke, Acts, and 2 Peter put the coming of Christ into the far distant future, and John and 1 John eliminate it by making it present in conversion. Or: Jesus intended neither a Church nor a hierarchy; but Jewish organizational principles entered the Church, and Acts, the Pastorals, and Ephesians all attest to an institutional, hierarchical Church. Braun goes on, but there is no need to follow him further. His point is clearly and forcefully made: scholars have shown that the New Testament contains such radical contradictions that it can no longer function as one "canon" or norm. In this radical form, Braun's thesis has not found many followers.

Please recall my disjunctions. Either the New Testament canon is authoritative, or it is not. Braun says it is not; the other theologians I will quote say it is. If it is authoritative, then its authority is affirmed by criteria that are either internal or external to itself. Internal criteria are either the whole of the Scripture or part of it.

The theologian who most typically affirms the authority of the Bible by appealing to the whole of the Bible is Karl Barth. Scripture, for Barth, is essentially a witness to divine revelation.[3] What validates the canon of Scripture, these books and no others, is that revelation, which, as Barth writes, "underlies and controls the Church, attests these witnesses and not others as the witnesses of revelation and therefore as canonical for the Church."[4] He can even say that the Holy Scripture forces itself upon the Church by its own inspiration.[5] "Every bit of real witness of God's revelation,"

---

[3] Barth, *The Doctrine of the Word of God*, 457.

[4] Ibid., 474.

[5] "But even though it is in and with the Church that we ask what is that Holy Scripture which is the Canon given in the Church and forcing itself upon it by its own inspiration, we cannot take our answer from the Church but from Holy Scripture itself" (ibid., 475).

Barth writes, is found in the sixty-six books of the canon.[6] For Barth, who shows a deeply religious reverence for the Bible, the Bible validates itself as the unique and complete witness to revelation.

Other theologians find the authority of the Bible confirmed by criteria that are internal to the Scriptures but comprise only a part of the Scriptures. This view is particularly typical of Lutherans, who follow Luther's hermeneutical principle of the dichotomy between Law and Gospel; the essence of Christianity is the proclamation of the Gospel.

Luther himself held that a book is canonical because it is evangelical—that is, because it proclaims Christ. In the famous "Preface to the Epistles of St. James and St. Jude," written in 1522, Luther stated: "all the genuine sacred books agree in this, that all of them preach and inculcate [*treiben*] Christ. And that is the true test by which to judge all books, when we see whether or not they inculcate Christ."[7]

The exegete Werner Georg Kümmel also makes the proclamation of Christ the real norm of the canon; he calls it the "inner norm."[8] Using this norm, one can refute "the appeal of Catholic or sectarian doctrines to certain single texts of the canon" with firmly grounded arguments. "We attain," he writes, "the freedom to understand the central proclamation of Christ in the New Testament in its different forms precisely as the *norm* upon which the Christian of every later age knows that he as a hearer depends, without having to fall into the temptation of recognizing *every* word of the New Testament as normative merely because it was received into the church's collection of apostolic writings." Hence, for Kümmel, there are passages in the New Testament that are not norma-

---

[6] "Every bit of real witness of God's revelation—we cannot without error deny the presence of such witness among the sixty-six books—is also a portion of God's Word and is all-sufficient for the life of the Church and for our own life in time and in eternity" (ibid., 476).

[7] *Luther's Works,* Vol. 35: *Word and Sacrament* I, ed. E. Theodore Bachmann (Philadelphia: Muhlenberg, 1960) 396.

[8] Werner Georg Kümmel, "Notwendigkeit und Grenze des neutestamentlichen Kanons," *Zeitschrift für Theologie und Kirche* 47 (1950) 277–313, repr. in idem, *Heilsgeschehen und Geschichte,* ed. E. Grässer et al. (Marburg: Elwert, 1965) 230–259; and in Käsemann, *Das Neue Testament als Kanon,* 62–97, here 96–97.

tive, because they do not proclaim Christ. Thus the final norm is not Scripture, but the proclamation of Christ.

Another exegete, Ernst Käsemann, judges that the "proclamation of Christ" is too vague as a norm and wants to specify the norm as "justification," which he says is the heart of the New Testament "Gospel" and the "canon within the canon." He writes that:

> the proclamation of justification appears to me indispensable as the qualifying and decisive criterion of the New Testament. Justification can function as such to the extent that, in historical exegesis, Jesus' distinguishing characteristic, in distinction to his entire religious environment, was association with sinners in God's name; that his crucifixion was decisively bound up with his shattering of the Law; and that association with sinners first made the mission to the Gentiles possible; and that the original Christian proclamation in general is more or less centrally determined by justification. Dogmatically, justification, more decisively than any other theological category, illuminates Christianity's understanding of God, man, and their mutual relations. Where this justification is no longer clearly and centrally proclaimed, there ends for me the theological authority of the canon along with what is specifically Christian.[9]

For Käsemann, "the Scripture remains distinct from the Gospel." The norm for truth in the Scripture is the Gospel, or the proclamation of justification; what does not proclaim justification may be in the Scripture, but it is not Gospel.

Thus some attempts to account for the authority of the canon by appealing to internal criteria, either the whole of the Scripture or part of it, such as the proclamation of Christ, or justification. Other theologians appeal to criteria that are external to the Scriptures. Some of them appeal to historical criteria. Their terms differ, but each of them says that the New Testament emerged at a time in the history of the Church that was privileged or unique because it was early.

For R.P.C. Hanson, for example, "between the years 100 and 150 the Church was in a position to know what were authentic and original records of Christianity and what were not; but as the years went on the Church inevitably found itself no longer in this

---

[9] Ernst Käsemann, "Kritische Analyse," in idem, *Das Neue Testament als Kanon,* 368–369.

position.''[10] The primary function of the New Testament is to serve as evidence, and the later the evidence, the less trustworthy it is. ''In forming the Canon of the New Testament the Church put itself under the authority of the New Testament's witness and abdicated its right (if it ever possessed such a thing) of adding to or subtracting from this witness.'' ''The formation of a Canon meant that the Church placed its teaching under this Canon, regarding it henceforward as its doctrinal norm.''[11]

For Oskar Cullmann, apostolic authorship, understood of a period of time rather than of individual writers, is the norm for the authority of the canon. Cullmann distinguishes apostolic from post-apostolic tradition as authentic from doubtful tradition. About the year 150, he writes, the Church established the principle of an apostolic canon and an apostolic summary of the kerygma, and thereby reestablished, for all time, its bond with the apostolic age. All tainted and misleading sources were excluded and all later tradition was submitted to judgment by the canon. ''Thus,'' Cullmann concludes, ''the Church made it possible for its members always to hear the original, apostolic word anew for all time— ever more, to experience the presence of Christ: a privilege that no oral tradition mediated by Polycarp or Papias could guarantee.''[12]

Hans von Campenhausen rejects apostolic authorship as a norm and speaks simply of the early date of the New Testament writings. He writes that the

> . . . view, dominant today, that the principle for deciding whether a work should be admitted into the New Testament was that of its authorship by an apostle, is devoid of all foundation. So far as any ''principle'' can be discerned behind the sources, it appears to be one simply of chronological limitation: the normative testimonies must derive from the period closest to Christ, namely that of Christian origins, the age of the apostles

[10] R.P.C. Hanson, *Tradition in the Early Church* (Philadelphia: Westminster, 1963) 234–235.

[11] Ibid.

[12] Oskar Cullmann, ''Die Tradition und die Festlegung des Kanons durch die Kirche des 2. Jahrhunderts,'' in idem, *Die Tradition als exegetisches, historisches und theologisches Problem* (Zurich: Zwingli, 1954) 42–54; repr. in Käsemann, *Das Neue Testament als Kanon*, 98–108, here 106–107.

and their disciples. This is in keeping with the "historical" character of the New Testament, and to a certain extent also with the
corresponding principle on which the Old Testament was defined within the Jewish synagogue.[13]

For Hanson, the New Testament is the Church's collection of
authentic and original evidence. For Cullmann, the New Testament is, in a broad sense, the apostolic writings. For Campenhausen, the New Testament contains the earliest Christian writings
we possess. Each appeals to a historical fact rather than to a theological principle. The question needs to be asked, whether historical data alone suffice to explain the Church's proclamation of the
twenty-seven books as uniquely the "word of the Lord."

Finally, among theologians who appeal to external criteria that
are dogmatic rather than historical, Karl Rahner is a good example.
It should be obvious that this position, which tries to relate the
canon of Scripture to the authority of the Church, is a typically
Catholic one.

Rahner affirms, as a foundational principle, that "scripture [is]
the church's book."[14] This phrase does not mean that the Church
creates Scripture, however, but that "scripture . . . is the objectification of the church of the apostolic age which is normative for
us."[15] Rahner states his view of the relation of Church and canon
in these—typically Rahnerian—sentences:

> During the apostolic age the real theological essence of the church
> is constituted in a historical process in which the church comes
> to the fullness of this essence and to the possession of this es-
> sence in faith. This self-constitution of the essence of the church
> until it reaches its full historical existence (and it is not until then
> that it can fully be the norm for the future church) implies writ-
> ten objectifications. Therefore this process is *also*, but not exclu-
> sively, the process of the formation of the canon: the church
> objectifies its faith and its life in written documents, and it recog-
> nizes these objectifications as so pure and so successful that they

---

[13] Hans von Campenhausen, *The Formation of the Christian Bible,* trans. J.
A. Baker (Philadelphia: Fortress, 1972) 330.

[14] Rahner, *Foundations,* 370.

[15] Ibid., 371.

are able to hand on the apostolic church as a norm for future ages.[16]

Rahner does the opposite of what most Protestant authors do: he does not say that the primitive Church—that is, the Church before the existence of the canon of the New Testament—was the ideal or normative Church. Instead, he sees Church and canon as both incomplete until they attain a certain relative independence, the ability to serve as critical norms for each other. If I may introduce a lowly image, he sees the formation of Church and canon as the division of one cell into two. The cell is unstable and in process until the division is accomplished; the two cells, after the division, complement each other. The formation of the New Testament writings is also a moment in the formation of the Church.

Another Catholic, Hans Küng, stated the position less complexly but rather more forcefully when he wrote:

> It is the *Church*, as the people of God of the New Testament, who has transmitted the New Testament to us; the history of the Canon does indeed include change, but all the same it is the New Testament as a *whole* that has been transmitted to us. Without the Church there would be no New Testament. Further, the Church's mind on the matter has definitely been that every part of the New Testament was included in the Canon as a positive witness to the Christ-event (and not to some extent as negative programmes for contrast's sake). It is true that it was the early Catholic Church that gave us the Canon. But that early Catholic Church proclaims her catholicity by the very fact that she did not exclude Paul, as an early Catholic Church would have to have done to be consistent in the sense of Protestant exegesis. But just by including Paul along with Acts, Paul along with James; by, in short, making the *whole* New Testament canonical, she carried out her "discernment of spirits." Catholic theology is of the opinion that she did it well and that we cannot do it any better today. The individual exegete cannot achieve his own discernment of spirits better than by trusting to that discernment of spirits which was carried out by the early Church and maintained by the later Church, and which has transmitted to us the New Testament as such.[17]

[16] Ibid., 373.

[17] Hans Küng, " 'Early Catholicism' in the New Testament as a Problem in Controversial Theology," in idem, *The Council in Action: Theological Reflec-*

When I was considering the concept of authority, I said that, because truth is by nature intelligible, all authority, even divine authority, can be authenticated; and thus the question of the authority of the Bible can and should be asked. In the theologians just surveyed, we have seen a search for the norm that authenticates the canon of Scripture. Braun denies that the canon is authoritative. For Barth, the whole canon is authoritative because it contains God's revelation, although not every word in the Bible is revelation. Kümmel and Käsemann, following Luther, shift attention from the canon to a norm that judges the canon and separates out the dross from the gold in the Bible, an approach that emphasizes the norm over the Scripture. Hanson, Cullmann, and von Campenhausen rest content with a historical norm: in essence, early date; but a historical criterion can yield only a historical result. Rahner sees the canon as the book in which the Church objectifies itself; neither Church nor canon is wholly objectified, and thus able to serve as the norm for the future Church, until they are distinct.

Each theologian searches for a norm to account for or validate the authority of Scripture. I find the line Rahner takes helpful. But one might go a bit further, and ask what norm guided the Church's objectification of itself in the canon. I propose that that norm is the rule of faith.

The Rule of Faith

The rule of faith was already mentioned in two other contexts.

The first was in connection with the problem of having four Gospels in the canon. The Muratorian Fragment proposed a solution to the problem, in these terms:

> And therefore, though various ideas are taught in the several books of the Gospels, yet it makes no difference to the faith of believers, since by one sovereign Spirit all things are declared in all of them concerning the Nativity, the Passion, the Resurrection, the conversation with his disciples and his two comings, the first in lowliness and contempt, which has come to pass, the second glorious and with royal power, which is to come.[18]

---

tions on the Second Vatican Council, trans. C. Hastings (New York: Sheed and Ward, 1963) 187.

[18] Cited from Stevenson, *A New Eusebius,* 145.

In its essential contours, this explanation was generally accepted, at least until the rise of historicism, in most of the Church.

The rule of faith was also mentioned when we considered Irenaeus's answer to the Gnostics on the problem of the right norm for interpreting the Scriptures. The Gnostics took their own cosmological principles as the right norms for interpreting the Scriptures: the metaphysical dualism of matter and spirit as good and evil, and the tripartite division of human souls into spirituals, psychics, and chthonics. Irenaeus maintains that the rule of faith is the right norm. His formulations of the rule of faith vary, but the outline is constant: belief in one God, the Father and creator; in Jesus the Christ, his Son; in the Holy Spirit; and in the historical incarnation of the Son, who is the second Adam, to deliver us from sin. Irenaeus goes even further, and writes that the rule would suffice even if there were no Scriptures; the barbarians who cannot read the Scriptures are saved by accepting the rule in their hearts.

"The rule of faith," or its equivalent, as a term and a concept, became significant at the end of the second century; it was particularly important to Irenaeus and Tertullian. Both authors had a New Testament, and both vigorously opposed heresy. Both realized that the Scriptures alone did not suffice for refuting heresy; their opponents could appeal to the Bible just as readily as they could. Both thus realized that they needed a norm for interpreting the Scriptures, and the norm they accepted was the rule of faith.

But the rule of faith, as a reality, began to function much earlier. Even the early letters of St. Paul attest to the existence of a normative Christian confession, the forerunner both of the rule of faith and of baptismal creeds.

The oldest and most basic of all Christian confessions is the short statement, "Jesus is Lord"—three words in English, two in Greek. In his Letter to the Philippians, Paul quotes a hymn that ends with this statement: ". . . that at the name of Jesus every knee should bow, in heaven and on earth and under the earth, and every tongue confess that Jesus Christ is Lord, to the glory of God the Father" (Phil 2:10-11). Paul himself invokes this creed at key places in two of his most important letters. In the Letter to the Romans he writes: "If you confess with your lips that Jesus is Lord and believe in your heart that God raised him from the dead, you will be saved" (Rom 10:9); and in the First Letter to the Corinthians: "Therefore I want you to understand that no one speaking by the Spirit of God ever says 'Jesus be cursed!' and no one can say 'Jesus is Lord' except by the Holy Spirit" (1 Cor 12:3). The account of the martyrdom of St. Polycarp, which dates from the middle of the second century, plays on this confession with noteworthy irony. After Polycarp has been arrested for being a Christian, the chief of the police says to him, "What harm is there in saying, 'Caesar is Lord'?"[19] Polycarp, and the readers of the document, know, of course, that there is great harm in saying it; for to say "Caesar is Lord" is to deny that "Jesus is Lord."

Besides the confession that "Jesus is Lord," the Church had other brief confessional statements, such as "Jesus is the Christ"[20] and "Jesus is the Son of God."[21]

Paul's First Letter to the Corinthians also contains another noteworthy confessional statement, which takes a different form. It is not exclusively Christological, but relates the one God, the Father, to the Lord, Jesus Christ, and both Father and Christ to all of creation and to the human race:

> Yet for us there is one God, the Father,
>   from whom are all things
>   and for whom we exist,
> and one Lord, Jesus Christ,
>   through whom are all things
>   and through whom we exist (1 Cor 8:6).

The passage that helped shape creedal statements more than any other, perhaps because such frequent and dramatic use was made of it, was the baptismal command at the end of St. Matthew's Gospel:

> And Jesus came and said to them, "All authority in heaven and on earth has been given to me. Go therefore and make disciples

[19] *Martyrdom of Polycarp* 8, 2.

[20] "Who is the liar but he who denies that Jesus is the Christ?" (1 John 2:22).

[21] For example: "And whenever the unclean spirits beheld him, they fell down before him and cried out, 'You are the Son of God' " (Mark 3:11); "Whoever confesses that Jesus is the Son of God, God abides in him, and he in God" (1 John 4:15); "Who is it that overcomes the world but he who believes that Jesus is the Son of God?" (1 John 5:5); and "I believe that Jesus Christ is the Son of God" (Acts 8:37, western text).

of all nations, baptizing them in the name of the Father and of the Son and of the Holy Spirit, teaching them to observe all that I have commanded you; and lo, I am with you always, to the close of the age" (Matt 28:18-20).

The writings of the Apostolic Fathers contain many short, creed-like statements, but make almost no appeal to a rule of faith. An exception is the author of *First Clement* who, around A.D. 96, appealed to "the norm of our tradition."[22]

The situation changed dramatically in the latter half of the second century. The Muratorian Fragment, written around 180, appeals to the rule of faith (without calling it that) as the norm for the unity of teaching in the four Gospels.[23]

Irenaeus and Tertullian work out an elaborate understanding of the significance and function of the "canon of truth" or "rule of faith." Tertullian writes that "the rule of faith is one everywhere, alone incapable of alteration and reform."[24] Irenaeus writes that "the Church . . . has received" this rule of faith "from the apostles and their disciples."[25] Tertullian, never one to stop half way, writes that

> this Rule, taught (as will be proved) by Christ, allows of no questions among us, except those which heresies introduce and which make heretics. Provided the essence of the Rule is not disturbed, you may seek and discuss as much as you like. . . . Faith is established in the Rule. There it has its law, and it wins salvation by keeping the law. . . . To know nothing against the Rule is to know everything.[26]

The rule originates with the Gospel itself, Tertullian writes, and existed long before even the oldest of heresies.[27] This one rule, for

---

[22] *First Clement* 7, 2.

[23] Quoted above.

[24] Tertullian, *On the Veiling of Virgins* 1, trans. J.N.D. Kelly, *Early Christian Creeds,* 3rd ed. (London: Longman, 1972) 86.

[25] Irenaeus, *Against the Heresies* 1, 10, 1 (SC 264, 154).

[26] Tertullian, *On the Prescription of Heretics* 13-14, trans. S. L. Greenslade in *Early Latin Theology,* LCC (Philadelphia: Westminster, 1956) 40.

[27] "That this rule of faith has come down to us from the beginning of the gospel, even before any of the older heretics, much more before Praxeas, a pretender of yesterday, will be apparent both from the lateness of date which

Irenaeus, suffices to prove all heretics wrong.[28]

When they come to formulate the rule, Irenaeus and Tertullian generally structure it around the triple name of the baptismal command, "Father, Son, and Holy Spirit," although they sometimes mention only Father and Son. In one passage, for example, Irenaeus writes of "one God almighty, who made all things by His Word . . . and Spirit . . .; He is the Father of our Lord Jesus Christ."[29] Elsewhere Irenaeus writes of "God, the Father, uncreated, beyond grasp, invisible, one God the maker of all; . . . the Word of God, the Son of God, Christ Jesus our Lord, . . . and . . . the Holy Spirit."[30] Two of Irenaeus's formulations were quoted above. Tertullian also has a succinct formulation:

> The rule of faith is one everywhere, alone incapable of alteration and reform—the rule which teaches us to believe in one God almighty, creator of the world, and His Son Jesus Christ, born from the Virgin Mary, crucified under Pontius Pilate, raised on the third day from the dead, taken up into heaven, now sitting on the Father's right hand, destined to come to judge the living and the dead through the resurrection of the flesh.[31]

Irenaeus's and Tertullian's doctrine on the rule of faith can be summarized in the statements that follow.[32] The "rule of faith" means both the norm that guides the Christian's faith and the Christian's beliefs as normative. It is equivalent to the whole teaching of the Church as that teaching was proclaimed by the apostles and the prophets and recorded in the Scriptures. The term "rule of faith" always refers to what is original, to what is established in

---

marks all heresies, and also from the absolutely novel character of our newfangled Praxeas." Tertullian, *Against Praxeas* 2, trans. Peter Holmes, ANF 3, 598.

[28] Irenaeus, *Against the Heresies* 1, 22, 1 (SC 264, 310).

[29] Ibid., 1, 22, 1 (SC 264, 308–310).

[30] Irenaeus, *Proof of the Apostolic Preaching* 6, trans. Joseph P. Smith, ACW 16 (Westminster: Newman, 1952) 51.

[31] Tertullian, *On the Veiling of Virgins* 1, trans. J.N.D. Kelly, *Early Christian Creeds,* 3rd ed. (London: Longmans, 1972) 86.

[32] For this summary see B. Hägglund, "Die Bedeutung der 'regula fidei' als Grundlage theologischer Aussagen," *Studia Theologica* 12 (1958) 1–44, and Joseph T. Lienhard, "Regula Fidei," *Westminster Dictionary of Christian Spirituality,* ed. Gordon S. Wakefield (Philadelphia: Westminster, 1983) 334–335.

and preserved by the Church as true—in other words, the truth itself that was proclaimed by the Lord and the apostles. The rule of faith has no fixed form; each writer adapted it to his immediate goals and intent. It is not identical with the creeds, nor with Scripture, although it cannot contradict Scripture. It is a guide to the authentic interpretation of Scripture. The rule of faith is tradition in the original sense of that word, that is, the faith that has been handed on from the beginning.

Historically, it was the rule of faith—or, more broadly, orthodox tradition—that guided the formation of the New Testament canon. For a century and a half the Church had no New Testament, but it confessed its faith. And then, once a New Testament was established, the rule of faith functioned as the norm for its right interpretation. Irenaeus and Tertullian were the first to appeal to the rule as a norm for interpretation, but hardly the last.

And, I believe, the rule of faith can serve the same function today. The rule of faith was the Church's guide from the beginning, and it is its best guide still.

Epilogue

Considering the canon of the Christian Bible gives rise to many questions. The Christian Bible has two parts: the Old Testament, which the Church took over from the Synagogue on the condition of its Christological interpretation, and the New Testament, which, as a canonical collection of Christian writings, is evident not much before A.D. 200. Behind all questions of detail stands the larger question of authority: who or what is the authoritative guarantee of Christian truth? The only absolute or unconditioned authority is Jesus Christ, the risen Lord. The Old Testament is authoritative as God's word to his Chosen People that led up to the Messiah, the Christ. The authority of Christ the Lord is also present in tradition, in handing down what he said and did. And those who handed down, first and foremost the apostles, also enjoyed authority. The authority of tradition is finally fixed, but not exclusively so, in the canon of Scripture.

The New Testament does not exist as a body sealed off from everything around it. It exists in the Church (but not under it), and as a unique and privileged moment of tradition.

The Bible exists in the Church. To ask, where in the Church does it exist? may at first sound naive; but it is not. The answer, I believe, is: it exists, first and most importantly, in worship. The words of the Bible are not proclaimed in worship on Sunday, and every day, because scholars have written books about them; scholars write books about the Bible because its words are proclaimed in the Church. Luke's beautiful account of the two disciples on the road to Emmaus is one of the earliest witnesses to the Eucharistic liturgy: first the Scripture is explained, and then bread is broken. Justin Martyr, writing in the middle of the second century, attests to the fixed pattern of reading from the Scripture, the Old Testament or the Gospels; the celebration of the Eucharist followed.

The first Scripture scholars were preachers: Origen preached his way through much of the Bible. But he also wrote commentaries. The division of homily and commentary has grown ever wider in the Church. Surely they have complemented each other. Preaching without study risks becoming pure emotionalism; study without preaching risks becoming mere philology. Homily and commentary are distinct; but if they should be permanently divorced from each other, the result would be disastrous.

My purpose, in these lectures, has been to try to elaborate a Catholic understanding of the complex relations among Bible, Church, and authority. If I have not failed completely, I give thanks to the one God and Father, who has proclaimed his saving Word, Jesus our Lord, through the Holy Spirit; to him be glory and honor forever.

Further Reading

Sources

The Apostolic Fathers. Trans. Kirsopp Lake. 2 vols. LCL. Cambridge: Harvard, and London: Heinemann, 1970–1975. (Orig. publ. 1912–1913.) (Complete, in Greek and English.)

The Apostolic Fathers. Ed. Jack N. Sparks. Nashville and New York: Thomas Nelson, 1978. (Complete translation.)

Charles, R. H., ed. *The Apocrypha and Pseudepigrapha of the Old Testament in English.* 2 vols. Oxford: Clarendon, 1913.

Early Christian Fathers. Ed. and trans. Cyril C. Richardson et al. LCC. Philadelphia: Westminster, 1953. (The Apostolic Fathers without the *Epistle of Barnabas* and the *Shepherd* of Hermas; Justin's *First Apology;* short selections from Irenaeus, *Against Heresies.*)

Early Christian Writings: The Apostolic Fathers. Trans. Maxwell Staniforth. New York: Viking Penguin, 1968. (The *Shepherd* of Hermas is not included.)

Flavius Josephus. Trans. H. St. J. Thackaray et al. 9 vols. LCL. Cambridge: Harvard, and London: Heinemann, 1926–1965. (Greek and English.)

Froehlich, Karlfried, ed. and trans. *Biblical Interpretation in the Early Church.* Sources of Early Christian Thought. Philadelphia: Fortress, 1984. (Ptolemy's *Letter to Flora* and other important ancient texts, Jewish and Christian.)

Grant, Robert M. *Second-Century Christianity: A Collection of Fragments.* London: SPCK, 1957. (Fragments of Heracleon, Papias, Marcion, and others.)

Hennecke, E., and W. Schneemelcher, eds. *New Testament Apocrypha*. Trans. R. McL. Wilson. 2 vols. London: SCM, 1963, 1965.

Irenaeus of Lyons. *Against Heresies*. Trans. Alexander Roberts and W. H. Rambaut. ANF 1. Repr. Grand Rapids: Eerdmans, 1973. (Orig. publ. 1885.) (The only complete English translation of *Against the Heresies*.)

_____. *Against the Heresies*. Trans. and annotated by Dominic J. Unger, revised by John J. Dillon. ACW 55. New York/Mahwah: Paulist, 1992. (Book 1, with extensive notes.)

James, Montague Rhodes. *The Apocryphal New Testament*. Oxford: Clarendon, 1924.

Justin Martyr. *Writings*. Trans. Thomas B. Falls. FC 6. New York: Christian Heritage, 1948.

The Mishnah. Trans. Herbert Danby. London: Oxford, 1938.

The Mishnah: A New Translation. Trans. Jacob Neusner. New Haven: Yale, 1988.

Philo. Trans. F. H. Colson and G. H. Whitaker. 10 vols. LCL. London: Heinemann, and New York: Putnam, 1929–1962. (Greek and English.)

Sadowski, Frank, ed. *The Church Fathers on the Bible: Selected Readings*. New York: Alba, 1987. (Many interesting passages, including Jerome and later writers.)

Schoedel, William R. *A Commentary on the Letters of Ignatius of Antioch*. Hermeneia. Philadelphia: Fortress, 1985.

Stevenson, J., ed. *A New Eusebius: Documents Illustrative of the History of the Church to A.D. 337*. London: SPCK, 1968. (Includes the Muratorian Fragment.)

Trigg, Joseph W. *Biblical Interpretation*. Message of the Fathers, 9. Wilmington: Glazier, 1988.

Vermes, G., trans. *The Dead Sea Scrolls in English*. 2nd ed. Baltimore: Penguin, 1975.

Literature

Balthasar, Hans Urs von. "God Is His Own Exegete." *Communio* 13 (1986) 280–287.

Barrett, C. K. "The Interpretation of the Old Testament in the New." In *Cambridge History of the Bible*, I: *From the Beginnings to Jerome*, ed. P. R. Ackroyd and C. F. Evans, 377–411. Cambridge: University Press, 1970.

Barth, Karl. *The Doctrine of the Word of God*. Church Dogmatics I, 2. Trans. G. T. Thomson and Harold Knight. Edinburgh: T & T Clark, 1956.

Beckwith, Roger T. "Formation of the Hebrew Bible." In Mulder, *Mikra*, 39–86.

_____. *The Old Testament Canon of the New Testament Church and Its Background in Early Judaism*. Grand Rapids: Eerdmans, 1985.

Bévenot, Maurice. "Scripture and Tradition in Catholic Theology." In Bruce, *Holy Book*, 171–185.

Bruce, F. F. *The Canon of Scripture*. Downers Grove: Intervarsity, 1988.

_____. "Scripture and Tradition in the New Testament." In idem, *Holy Book*, 68–93.

_____, and E. G. Rupp, ed. *Holy Book and Holy Tradition: International Colloquium Held in the Faculty of Theology, University of Manchester*. Manchester: Manchester U. P., 1968.

Burtchaell, James Tunstead. *Catholic Theories of Biblical Inspiration since 1810: A Review and Critique*. Cambridge: Cambridge U. P., 1969.

Campenhausen, Hans von. *The Formation of the Christian Bible*. Trans. J. A. Baker. Philadelphia: Fortress, 1972.

Congar, Yves. "The Historical Development of Authority in the Church. Points for Reflection." In Todd, *Problems of Authority*, 119–156.

Crouzel, Henri. *Origen*. Trans. A. S. Worrall. San Francisco: Harper & Row, 1989.

Dodd, C. H. *According to the Scriptures: The Sub-Structure of New Testament Theology*. London: Collins, 1965. (First published 1952.)

_____. *The Authority of the Bible*. Rev. ed. Harper Torchbooks. New York: Harper & Brothers, 1960. (First edition 1929.)

_____. *The Old Testament in the New*. Rev. ed. Facet Books, Biblical Series, 3. Philadelphia: Fortress, 1965.

Ebeling, Gerhard. "The New Testament and the Multiplicity of Confessions." In idem, *The Word of God and Tradition: Historical Studies Interpreting the Divisions of Christianity*, trans. S. H. Hook, 148–159. Philadelphia: Fortress, 1968.

Farkasfalvy, Denis. "The Case for Spiritual Exegesis." *Communio* 10 (1983) 332–350.

_____. "In Search of a 'Post-Critical' Method of Biblical Interpretation for Catholic Theology." *Communio* 13 (1986) 288–307.

Flesseman-van Leer, Ellen. "Present-day Frontiers in the Discussion about Tradition." In Bruce, *Holy Book,* 154–170.

Gamble, Harry Y. *The New Testament Canon: Its Making and Meaning.* Philadelphia: Fortress, 1985.

Gnuse, Robert. *The Authority of the Bible: Theories of Inspiration, Revelation and the Canon of Scripture.* New York/Mahwah: Paulist, 1985.

Hanson, Richard C. *Tradition in the Early Church.* Philadelphia: Westminster, 1963.

Harnack, Adolf von. *Marcion: The Gospel of the Alien God.* Trans. John E. Steely and Lyle D. Bierma. Durham: Labyrinth, 1990.

Hoffman, Thomas. "Inspiration, Normativeness, Canonicity, and the Unique Sacred Character of the Bible." *Catholic Biblical Quarterly* 44 (1982) 447–469.

Horbury, William. "Old Testament Interpretation in the Writings of the Church Fathers." In Mulder, *Mikra,* 727–789.

Käsemann, Ernst. "The Canon of the New Testament and the Unity of the Church." In idem, *Essays on New Testament Themes,* trans. W. J. Montague, 95–107. Studies in Biblical Theology 41. Naperville: Allenson, 1964.

Kedar, Benjamin. "The Latin Translations." In Mulder, *Mikra,* 299–338.

Kelly, J.N.D. *Early Christian Creeds.* 3rd ed. London: Longman, 1972.

Kelly, Joseph F. *Why Is There a New Testament?* Wilmington: Glazier, 1986.

Kemmer, Alfons. *The Creed in the Gospels: An Introduction to the Biblical Sources of the Creed.* New York/Mahwah: Paulist, 1986.

Kereszty, Roch A. "The 'Bible and Christology' Document of the Biblical Commission." *Communio* 13 (1986) 342–367.

Kugel, James L., and Rowan A. Greer. *Early Biblical Interpretation.* Philadelphia: Westminster, 1986.

Küng, Hans. " 'Early Catholicism' in the New Testament as a Problem in Controversial Theology." In idem, *The Council in Action: Theological Reflections on the Second Vatican Council,* trans. C. Hastings, 159–195. New York: Sheed and Ward, 1963.